A CONTINUATION

OF THE

MEMOIRS

OF

A WORKING MAN;

ILLUSTRATED BY SOME

ORIGINAL SKETCHES OF CHARACTER.

"Still raise for good the supplicating voice,
But leave to Heav'n the measure and the choice."

LONDON:

CHARLES COX, 12, KING WILLIAM STREET,
STRAND.

1850.

PRINTED BY W. CLOWES AND SONS, STAMFORD STREET.

PREFACE.

THE favourable reception given to the 'Memoirs of a Working Man,' both by reviewers and general readers, naturally gave me much pleasure; and the more so, because I had not looked for such cordial approbation. I was thereby led to consider whether or not it would be advisable to write a 'Continuation' of these Memoirs. The result was, that I resolved to do so, if I were sanctioned by those upon whose judgment I could depend.

My judicious and disinterested patrons encouraged me to carry out my purpose, and I was the more disposed to act upon their advice, since in some of the published notices of the 'Memoirs,' as well as in several private communications, there was an expression of regret that I had not been somewhat more explicit upon several points connected with my personal history. Thus, being desirous of supplying what was felt to be wanting, and having, moreover, the full concurrence of my honoured patrons, I went to work; and, at length, have brought my humble labours to a close. If what is now offered to the reader should prove as acceptable as were the 'Memoirs,' I shall have renewed cause for gratitude and self-gratulation.

A CONTINUATION

OF THE

MEMOIRS OF A WORKING MAN.

CHAPTER I.

The 'Memoirs of a Working Man' were intended to have been published by subscription; for I had no hope that any one of my humble productions would find its way into print by the usual means. As to publishing on my own responsibility, this was wholly out of the question. I should not have dared to employ a printer, even if I could have found one who would have been willing to take such inadequate security for payment as alone I could have offered. Meanwhile the list of subscribers was so short as to be not a little discouraging, and I had much reason to fear that it would become yet more brief.

Several of the kind hearted patrons who had aided me on a similar occasion were either deceased, or had removed far away from their former homes; while my broken health, by preventing my going in search of additional subscribers, precluded all hope of my being enabled to repair the loss which I had sustained.

In this perplexity, as I was slowly threading my way through the crowded and noisy thoroughfare near St. Paul's Cathedral, with thoughts intent upon the subject of my seemingly useless manuscript, I was suddenly led to think that it might be well to wait upon a very worthy and kindhearted gentleman, from whom I had formerly received both good advice and valuable patronage. I forthwith obeyed the impulse; and, on reaching my patron's house, had the pleasure of finding him at home. He gave me a most courteous reception, so that I was encouraged to tell him the whole story of my literary troubles, as also of some other matters; and his kindness, together with the full confidence that I felt in his judgment and taste, led me to request that he would look over what I had written. I freely told him that he would find it made up of all sorts of "odds and ends," forming altogether a very heterogeneous mass. He at once assented to my request, and I took my leave of him with far more cheerful feelings than I otherwise should have enjoyed, especially on a dreary and gloom-engendering day in that month which is supposed by some of our lighthearted neighbours on the other side of the Channel to have a peculiarly depressing influence upon the animal spirits of Englishmen.

I lost no time in putting the manuscript into the hands of my patron. It was not long before it was returned with a note, from which the following is an extract:—"Do you not think you could contrive to give all the interesting events and thoughts in a much more condensed shape?"

I immediately resolved to act upon this suggestion, and returned an answer to that effect. Without delay I set about my task, and far more cheerfully than I am able to express. Suffice it to say, that I was "right glad of heart" at the prospect which thus unexpectedly had opened upon me. So that I could but sell my manuscript, I cared not about either the labour or the difficulty which I perceived would be involved in adapting it to the required ends. I now greatly felt the need of what has been pleasantly called "a literary condenser," as I could not but suspect my power to make a judicious abridgment; while I had much reason to fear, that a writer so habitually prolix as myself would be unable to compress the history of above twenty-nine years within any moderate compass,* unless at the expense of

* The MS. did not bring down my narrative to a later date than to the close of the year 1815. The history of the

making the narrative little better than a mere catalogue or chronicle.

Yet I was not hereby discouraged, for, in addition to my natural unwillingness to shrink from a task because of its difficulty or its toilsomeness, I was in this instance spurred on

"By the strong hand of stern necessity;"

being at the time unusually perplexed in regard to finding the means of meeting several pressing demands for money; while my pocket was in much the same state as the bag concerning which "Poor Richard" has said that "it is hard to make it stand upright." The hope, therefore, of being enabled to replenish it, drove far away all considerations of the labour, either physical or mental, which I might have to undergo in the prosecution of my work.

My health was, indeed, very infirm; the season of the year was not favourable to an asthmatic invalid; and I had to attend daily to other and imperative duties. All these hindrances, however, I regarded without much anxiety, because I hoped that some greatly needed and substantial good might accrue to my family if I duly executed my allotted task.

I was further animated by a belief that I should

following years was intended to have formed the subject of a subsequent volume.

in this, as in many previous instances, be favoured with as much " strength " as would render me equal to my necessities, whether of body or mind. So I forthwith set about my work; and here it may not be amiss if I give a brief account of the manner in which I prosecuted it. The history of one day will suffice for all, except at such times as I was more than usually unwell; when the scene of my operations was changed to my bed-room, and, instead of writing at a table, I wrote in bed.

As I then slept very ill, I was usually not a little weary of the night; and consequently had been driven to several expedients for whiling away its tedious hours. I was therefore not unwilling to find a fair occasion for rising very early, and I now generally did so, seldom being in bed later than four o'clock A.M. My great susceptibility of cold, and other infirmities, rendered a fire and some other accommodations necessary immediately after I arose; and as I could not allow myself to disturb any one at so unseasonable an hour, I provided them for myself, and then went to work. By breakfast-time I had usually got through a fair portion of my task. After breakfast I commenced my daily occupation of tailoring and other employments, among which was that of educating my youngest son; and also held myself in readiness to meet any other demands which might be made upon my time or attention. These very often were not a few, while they usually involved a considerable amount of anxiety or perplexity, most of them having relation to the immediate wants of my needy household. While thus employed I had but little time to give to my literary task, yet I did what I could; I took it in hand whenever I had a respite from my other duties; and thus generally made some progress in it during the day. I had to encounter one serious hindrance which I could not possibly avoid. This arose from my being forced to take an hour's rest in the afternoon of each day, in order to recover from the weariness and feebleness which never failed to come upon me soon after noontide. After this I was commonly somewhat more fit for both thinking and acting. When I had got through all my other business, I again gave my undivided attention to my manuscript; and by the time that I put it aside it had usually received some considerable amount of rather severe treatment, page after page having been wholly cancelled, closely written pages reduced to brief paragraphs, and long paragraphs melted down into short sentences.

Sometimes I felt, as may well be imagined by any one, but especially by an author of my class, a not unnatural twinge at seeing so much of what I had long and painfully worked at thus mercilessly dealt with; and that too by him from whom, as being his own progeny, it might seem to have deserved milder treatment. Yet the necessity of the case served to reconcile me to the pain involved in making these excisions and compressions. I therefore went on with them resolutely, until I had gone through the whole of the manuscript. When this was done, I could not but be a little touched at seeing the greatly reduced proportions of my once portly, if not rather overgrown offspring. Yet I ventured to hope that this reduction in its bulk might have added to its value, and thus have made it better fitted than it before was to answer the purposes of the worthy publisher. I did not preserve the rejected matter, but it is pretty well fixed upon my memory, and therefore can be easily brought into use, should its publication in another form appear to be advisable. It may not be superfluous here to state, that my having written so much not immediately relating to my personal history was caused by my having originally intended to connect with the 'Memoirs' such observations as I had made upon men and things in the course of my past life. Subsequently I was under a pledge to that effect, by means of a prospectus, in which the proposed book was announced under the title of 'The Life and Opinions of a Working Man.' In accordance, therefore, both with my original plan and my recorded pledge, I interwove with the web of my own history not a little of what had no immediate or necessary connection with it; and thus opinions were inserted concerning both public men and public transactions, as also concerning many other persons and things.

These were not mere notions taken up at random or at secondhand, but were really opinions, since they were the result of much previous observation and consideration.

I do not, however, vouch for their correctness; on the contrary, I am disposed to believe that in some of them I may have come to wrong conclusions, although the premises might have been correct; while in others I may have reasoned upon unsound principles, and consequently my decisions, although fair and just, are of no authority. I will only add, that I do not wish to dogmatise upon any question, much less do I wish to make converts to my individual opinions. I am not *now* so confident upon doubtful subjects as I was in danger of being when I was something more than thirty years younger than I now am. But while I thus mistrust my own judgment, I confess that I do not feel inclined to yield either an immediate or a full assent to that of others, unless they have claims to deference which I cannot question. I cannot answer for the constitution or temper of other men's minds; but in my own case there seems to be an insurmountable obstacle in the way of receiving any proposition or doctrine as just or true, until I have to the best of my ability considered the principles or reasons upon which it is said to be founded. If these appear to be solid, I have then no difficulty in renouncing my former opinions, and giving my ready and cordial assent to what has been propounded. But I do not even here feel at liberty to be quite positive as to its general and entire truthfulness. It is enough for me to know that I have done my best towards coming to a right conclusion.

Thus far I have referred to questions connected with merely *secular* affairs. In *religious* matters I am the subject of a somewhat different order of impressions. For example, in all that relates to the Christian faith, whether it be doctrinal or preceptive, I feel no difficulty in giving it my ready and full credence upon the bare authority of the Scriptures. But even in these cases I should probably hesitate, had I not (as I have done) used every available means of being enabled to judge of the authenticity and the genuineness of these records. I have long had a full and steady belief in their Divine origin, and, consequently, in their truthfulness and authority. Thus, I am ever ready to receive their announcements—whether they relate to faith or to practice—provided only that I be allowed to understand them according to their plain and literal meaning; as I cannot easily take them with a gloss, however ingenious or plausible.

But I must leave this subject, and proceed with

what remains to be told concerning the completion of my manuscript. The *printed* 'Memoirs' consist of two hundred and thirty-four pages. Of these, the original manuscript furnished matter for one hundred and eighty-two, including, however, the Title-page, Introduction, and Preface; thus leaving me but fifty-four pages whereon to inscribe an account of events stretching over not less than twenty-nine years. As these years of my life were far more full of incidents than were the preceding twenty-two, I felt, all the more, the difficulty involved in giving such a history of them as would be likely to prove satisfactory. It was indispensable that I should be concise, and therefore that I should select such incidents for my record as might seem to have the chief claim upon my notice. This, however, was a rather perplexing task; yet I went to work resolutely; and *now*, upon reviewing what I selected, I know not that I could have done better. Nevertheless, since the completion of the manuscript, I have remembered a good many things which, I think, might be acceptable to the readers of the 'Memoirs.' Of some of these I shall probably take a little notice in the following pages.

After I had finished the labour of recasting and completing the manuscript, I forthwith sent it to my patron, and then endeavoured to be duly prepared for whatever might be the issue. But I dare not affirm that I was unconscious of any anxiety; on the contrary, I freely confess to have felt a very deep and earnest concern about it. In good truth, it was—to me and mine—a question of no trifling or common interest.

My health was at the time greatly impaired; our little business was not nearly equal to the supply of our unavoidable wants; while some pecuniary obligations pressed for immediate discharge. My household alternated between hope and fear—the latter emotion, however, greatly preponderating. Thus, notwithstanding whatever might have been my own misgivings, it became necessary that I should sometimes imitate those who are said to

"Affect a virtue though they have it not,"

and thus endeavour to wear the aspect, and to use the language, of one who had but little fear that the issue would be unsatisfactory.

In truth, I really had some considerable degree of hope as to the result. I could not but regard the whole matter, so far as it had gone, as having been under the control and direction of Divine Providence; because, on looking at it soberly, I seemed to have been actuated by worthy motives in preparing the manuscript. I was further encouraged because I remembered the good success of my former humble attempts at authorship, both in regard to the approbation of my patrons and the relief of my necessities.

Meanwhile I did not fail to do all that was practicable towards providing for the support of myself and family. In regard to literary occupation I was not idle; as I had intimated, at the close of the 'Memoirs,' that I should forthwith commence another work, and, moreover, was desirous of not losing the pleasure which, in my case, is usually attendant upon literary composition. I therefore began, without even a day's intermission, to do something towards finishing a little work which had long been in abeyance, but which I much wished to complete. I gave my attention to it whenever I had leisure for the purpose, and was able to use a pen. It is, however, still in an unfinished state, having been put aside when I began to write these pages.

I made no inquiry about the manuscript, being of opinion that, whatever might be the result, the news would arrive in due time. Good news is never the worse for being a little tardy in its approach; while, as regards evil tidings, we seldom have cause to complain that they have lingered on their way. After the lapse of a few weeks I learned that the question was settled. At the close of a dark, wintry day, when I was, somewhat gravely, musing upon other matters, a sharp and quick double-rap at the door announced the arrival of one who has been aptly described as the

> "messenger of grief
> Perhaps to thousands, and of joy to some."

To us he had sometimes been the bearer of disastrous or otherwise unwelcome tidings, but on this occasion he was the herald of good. That this would prove to be the case was conjectured before opening the packet, which, from its size and shape, gave intimation that it was not any ordinary communication. Yet no one ventured even so much as a conjecture as to what it actually was. On opening it there appeared a printed paper and a written note. The first was a proof-sheet of the 'Memoirs,' while the second contained a request that the text might not be altered, but that my corrections should be wholly confined to typographical errors.

The pleasurable change in our feelings of which we all were now conscious may be more easily imagined than described. As to myself, all my anxiety about the affair was now at an end. I felt that I was relieved of no small burden of domestic trouble, and could not but rejoice that the cloud which, for a good while, had been gathering around us, was partially dispersed, and that a comparatively bright season was at hand.

When I found that Mr. Knight had written an Introduction to my little book, I was additionally gratified, because I felt assured that it would, in some way or other, contribute to my advantage;

but after I had read it, I was sensible that it laid me under an amount of obligation to that gentleman which it would be difficult fully to express, and which, moreover, it would be impossible to discharge. I could not but be sensibly moved by the singularly generous and kind spirit in which it had evidently been written; while, as to its propitious influence upon the success of the volume I could not entertain a doubt.

The tenor of the directions given me, in regard to correcting the proof-sheet, served yet further to cheer me, because they led me to conclude that I had fully met my patron's wishes relative to the revision and completion of the manuscript. To finish this long story, I will merely add that I gave my most earnest attention to the whole of the correcting process, and then, with some eagerness of expectation, looked for the appearance of my rather diminutive book among its more full-grown compeers of the Weekly Volumes. As I had now done all that devolved upon me in regard thereto, I was so far contented. It then occurred to me that I would review all the circumstances connected with its progress and completion; on doing which I was fully convinced that I owed nothing to the agency of

"that fickle power—
If power she be—that works but to confound."

Thus my long-entertained and deeply-rooted incredulity concerning what are called fortuitous or accidental events, was yet further strengthened; while I felt encouraged to adopt the sentiment of the quaint, yet expressive, and, as I think, finely-conceived proverb, "He who observes a Providence shall never want a Providence to observe;" and to this truly wise saying to add another, of especial interest to myself, "God's providence is man's inheritance."

The subject which next engaged the thoughts of both myself and my family was that of the reception which the 'Memoirs' would meet with from the reviewers. My wife and children, as was quite natural on *their* parts, were of opinion that the book deserved to be noticed in a friendly, if not in a highly commendatory, manner. For myself, as I had been formerly noticed on more than one occasion by a goodly number of critics, each of whom gave to my little publications the expression of his hearty approbation, I ventured to hope that in *this* instance I should not be left without, at least, some encouraging amount of critical favour and commendation.

Nor was this hope either disappointed or long deferred; for I soon received a copy of the current number of the 'Inquirer' newspaper, which contained a notice of the 'Memoirs.' This notice, although brief, was to me of a very gratifying character, inasmuch as it bore unequivocal testimony to the useful tendency of my otherwise unimportant book; and it was the more satisfactory because it pointed out some of the chief grounds upon which this good tendency was considered to rest, one of which was that of its inculcating principles and habits that serve to promote the interests of both moral and physical order. I was heartily glad of this, because I have long believed that

"Order is Heaven's first law."*

Of this, indeed, I think few can have any serious doubt, provided that they have observed either the evils which are connected with the neglect of this virtue, or the great benefits flowing from a due obedience to its claims. For myself, I am constrained to believe that the well-being of man, considered either individually or collectively, is chiefly dependent upon his willing and consistent obedience to the "laws of order;" and further, that the sum total of human happiness or misery

* Every competent observer of either the natural or the moral world will readily subscribe to the doctrine inculcated in this quotation. It were superfluous to adduce any laboured proofs from the former, in which "arrangement neat and chastest order" are everywhere to be seen; while as regards the latter, notwithstanding the disturbing influence of an antagonist principle, there is evidence sufficient to satisfy every candid person that it—

"moves on
In higher order, fitted and impell'd
By wisdom's finest hand, and issuing all
In general good."

is, and ever must be, in exact proportion to the amount of this obedience. In passing, I venture to observe that I am forced to suspect there is some defect either in the intellect or in the moral sense of all who are indifferent or negligent concerning habits of external order, whether it be in their persons or in the management of their concerns.*

I must, however, dismiss these reflections for the purpose of acknowledging my obligations to another friendly critic, who, in the 'Apprentice' of the same date as the 'Inquirer,' viz. February 22, 1845, has dwelt at considerable length, and with much kindheartedness, upon the 'Memoirs' and their author. This gentleman wishes that I had been more explicit upon matters wherein the affec-

* My son, whose decease is recorded at page 226 of the 'Memoirs,' was remarkable for his early and continued exemplification of the good which results from a love of order. I still preserve, in just the same state in which he left them, some little articles of which he was the owner. These alone would suffice to show that he loved to be orderly and exact even in trifles; but for any one fully to appreciate his character in this respect, it were needful to have been personally acquainted with his disposition and habits. For his sake I may not mourn over my bereavement, but rather am bound to rejoice that one so well fitted for that world where all that is disorderly or confused is unknown, should, although at so early an age, have been removed thither. It were easy for me to enlarge upon this topic, but, at present, I must not allow myself that indulgence.

tions are chiefly engaged. To this I would answer that I could very easily have been so; as I have had much to do with circumstances and incidents that came home very closely to the heart, and were adapted to awaken its tenderest sympathies. But I refrained, first, because there was, after all, nothing extraordinary connected with my cares or sorrows; secondly, because I wished to avoid the manifestation of a mawkish or sickly sensibility; and thirdly, because I am susceptible of feelings, when under the pressure of trouble or sadness, which I suspect to be, in a great measure, peculiar to myself, and which, therefore, could not readily be so explained as to make their history greatly interesting, if indeed intelligible, to the generality of readers. I will, however, observe that they are of so quieting a character as that I could wish them to be understood, and (in the hour of want or of sorrow) be also possessed by every human being.

But I must not linger here, as I wish to tell my very friendly reviewer of some little matters with which, I think, he may at least be amused. Were it convenient, I should try to obtain a personal interview with him, as I then could be more explicit upon several points than I can venture to be through the medium of the press. I can assure him that a critical notice, such as his, of the 'Memoirs,' is of no trifling value to one who, although he is an occasional writer of books, is far enough from the vanity of assuming to be a literary man. How much I have been cheered by his encouraging observations, as to the useful tendency of my little book, I cannot duly express. Glad, indeed, should I be were I to know that my fellow-craftsmen have derived from the 'Memoirs' all that mental and moral good which this gentleman believes such publications are adapted to be the instruments of communicating. I bear willing testimony to the large amount of intellectual power and the very creditable acquirements of many among my fellow-workmen;* but I must not conceal the humiliating fact, that these otherwise superior men are commonly very deficient in regard to moral feeling, and, consequently, lamentably negligent of moral duties and obligations. Most of them pay no regard whatever to the Sunday; that day, invaluable as it is as a day of bodily rest, of mental instruction, and of moral amelioration, is either spent in working, wasted in listlessness, or prostituted to the purposes of grossly sensual pleasure. The few who give any attention to religious questions are, with but few exceptions, either sceptics,

* With regard to some of these men I can also speak as to their power of perceiving and enjoying the qualities of beauty and sublimity, whether in the works of nature or of art, but in each of these cases the good taste of the individual was thrown into the shade by his frequent indulgence in what was either thoroughly vulgar or grossly immoral.

or decided and reckless unbelievers; while, among the still smaller number who profess to be religious men, there are not wanting such as, by their inconsistent lives, give ample occasion for " stumbling " to unstable minds; and, moreover, greatly to confirm their doubting or infidel brethren in their respective errors.* These are facts which I record with much reluctance, but which I dare not even attempt to conceal, especially as I entertain a hope that the full avowal of them by one who, like myself, knows that they cannot be successfully controverted, may lead to some useful result.

As this friendly critic has so warmly commended me for darning my " stockings and body linen," perhaps it may not be amiss if I inform him that not very long ago, during the sleepless hours of my wearisome nights, in the winter season, I employed myself in knitting. As I had found myself unable in those hours either to sew, write, or read, I knew not what I could contrive in order to escape from the great misery

---

* I must here note, that I have met with scarcely one of these professed unbelievers who had taken the trouble to make himself fairly acquainted with the contents of the Bible; consequently they have nothing to advance against its announcements, save what is of the most vague or inconclusive character. It has sometimes fallen to my lot to see them brought to a stand on being requested to verify their suppositious or garbled quotations from the Scriptures by a direct reference to the text.

of being wholly unemployed. At length I bethought me that I would try how far I could get on in the manufacture of a stocking. I was not very confident in my hopes of success, for I had done nothing in this way for nearly forty years; yet I resolved to make the attempt, and was well pleased to discover that I could make better progress than I had anticipated. The issue was, that I not only had such employment as enabled me to get through many a long night with comparative comfort, but also that I succeeded so well as to become the owner of two pair of stockings of my own manufacture,* which I have found to be both convenient and useful. I ought perhaps to add, that knitting seems to be the only occupation which I can follow at night, without distressing either the eyes or the organs of respiration. It were indeed nearly impossible by such an employment to procure the means of subsistence, even of the most humble description; yet, although of but little worth to

---

* Thus I was far better supplied than before with some very necessary articles of clothing, and was further confirmed in the belief of an instructive proverb which my good mother had often repeated in my hearing—"A thing well learned is never forgot." Here, however, I must be allowed to make a brief reflection. If this saying is in agreement with facts, it follows that all possible care should be taken to avoid learning whatever is not in strict harmony with genuine goodness and truth.

any healthy and active person, it is not undeserving of attention on the part of an invalid, to whom it is at least better than no occupation; inasmuch as it serves to keep him from the depressing influence of total inactivity.

Before I take my leave of the gentleman to whom the preceding remarks are addressed, I ought to let him know that I have been allowed "the privilege of admission to the Reading-room at the British Museum" during the last seven years—a privilege I highly value, but of which I can very rarely avail myself, as I have neither the leisure nor the bodily vigour necessary for that purpose. My visits have been chiefly on behalf of a gentleman who requested me to assist him in his endeavours to meet with some lyrical compositions, of which he wished to have a little further knowledge. I obtained admission through the interposition of a gentleman, well known and justly honoured in the literary world, to whose generous and unwearied patronage I owe numerous obligations. When I last removed from my native town, it was with the fixed purpose of setting myself down in some place adjacent to the residence of my honoured patron; but my intention was altogether frustrated; for I was unavoidably (and, at the time, almost unaccountably) led to take up my abode in a little tenement on the south side of the Thames, at a distance of several miles from the neighbourhood in which I had intended to dwell. I looked on this however as but a temporary arrangement; nevertheless, it was otherwise ordered; and this cottage, which, in several respects, is far from being desirable, has hitherto been our constant dwelling-place. Yet, notwithstanding its inconveniences, we are unwilling to leave it because there is attached to it a small piece of gardenground, in the cultivation of which my good partner, who is fond of flowers and plants, finds pleasure, and where I sometimes get " a peep at nature," with which, but for this, I could not be indulged. Another attraction is, that the neighbourhood is tolerably reputable and orderly. But I find my strongest inducement to stay where I am in a growing dislike and dread of change. I am now more than ever of Poor Richard's opinion, that " three removes are as bad as a fire," and further, that " a rolling stone gathers no moss." I have already removed more than three times, and have no wish to repeat the unwelcome process. As to the " moss," it is indeed quite true that, in this case, the " stone" has not gathered much, although it has for so long a time avoided " rolling;" but the failure is easily accounted for by the fact that it has been continually acted upon by the forceful waters of adversity, and thus has been prevented from accumulating anything. It might, perhaps, be safely affirmed that the "stone" itself has suffered some loss of bulk by the ceaseless action of these unpropitious currents.

Here I am led to observe that my having been induced to settle upon the southern side of the Thames, instead of the northern, as I had intended, was, I doubt not, ordered by Him, whose providence governs the affairs of men, and "fixes the bounds of their habitations." I have learned, by experience, that the air in the northern suburbs of London is, in general, much too cold and sharp for my over-sensitive frame, which requires a milder and a somewhat medicated atmosphere; I seem to get this on the southern side of the metropolis, and thus am more willing to put up with the inconvenience of living so far distant from the places to which my business frequently calls me.

But I must now say farewell to my friendly critic of the 'Apprentice;' merely adding that, if he should look through this little book, he will find some further intimations concerning both myself and my dwelling-place.

I now come to make a few remarks upon what is said of the "Working Man" in the 'British Friend of India Magazine' for March, 1845. The notice is a short one, but I do not, on that account, place less value upon the testimony it bears to the useful tendency of the book. What is there said concerning myself cannot but be gratifying to my feelings, while it may well encourage me to make further efforts on the behalf of others.

It is strictly true that I have, through the whole course of my life, felt "strong aspirations after knowledge." For this tendency of mind I am grateful to Him who is the only fountain of all true intelligence; but I am far more thankful for having been led, by the same gracious Being, to see something of the beauty of virtue, and to feel somewhat of the force of virtuous principles. But for his secret yet powerful influence, I had learned nothing of moral virtue, nor felt any inclination to obey the dictates of Christian morality. The reviewer will allow me to thank him for his expressions of sympathy in regard to my "struggles to provide things honest in the sight of men." He may rest assured that he has not gone beyond the truth in applying to those struggles the epithet of "zealous," as I can safely affirm that nothing has ever weighed heavier upon my heart than has the consciousness of not being able duly to pay every one the amount of his just demands.

It would perhaps seem like self-commendation were I to go into detail respecting the contrivances that were resorted to and the privations that were endured, both by myself and my ever-anxious wife, in order that we might, as far as was possible, keep out of debt. But my continuous ill-health and consequent feebleness effectually prevented the accomplishment of our earnest purpose; nor could we recover the ground we had already lost. I fear, however, even seeming to complain of either my bodily affliction or the embarrassments consequent thereon; and therefore will not enlarge upon these topics. I had much rather find cause for gratitude to the " Father of all mercies," and, happily, I need not look long for this, since I have never been left without hope, nor (for any very long time) without help. Although this help was not at all equal to my necessities, yet it was the means of preventing my being wholly overwhelmed by the " sea of troubles" upon which I was, at the time, drifting along, without the power of directing my seemingly perilous course.

I here record, with unaffected gratitude to God, the fact of my having been enabled, amidst all my worldly difficulties, to retain the character of an honest and well-intending man. That my creditors believed me to be so is evident from the fact of my having received, not only the expression of sympathy from all of them, but also pecuniary help from nearly all, in more than one season of severe affliction, and, consequently, of urgent necessity. Should these considerate and generous men learn what is here recorded, I beg them to believe that the writer yet retains, and hopes ever to retain, a very lively sense both of their kindness and of his obligations.

The next in order of the reviews of the 'Memoirs' is that which appeared in the 'Weekly Dispatch' newspaper of March 23rd, 1845. It deserves, and, with but one exception, it has, my cordial and full approbation. I tender my hearty thanks to the reviewer for his commendation of my book, and for the generous sympathy which he manifests towards its author. He will, unless I greatly mistake his temper, allow me freely to express my dissent from the sentiment of the passage in which he speaks of the writer of the 'Memoirs' as having been, in common with many others of his class, " totally unrewarded either by man or Heaven." I may not confidently pronounce upon what may have been the experience of others, but for myself, I am bound to say, that were I to be querulous I should be greatly and inexcusably culpable; for in many an otherwise comfortless hour of trouble or of sickness I have been favoured with the kind and active sympathy of one or another of my fellow-men; while,

" By the mercy of indulgent Heaven,"

I have been not only sustained, but animated and comforted. These human sympathies, and, as I fully believe them to be, heavenly consolations, I regard as a good compensation for the loss of worldly prosperity and bodily health, while I hardly need say that they afforded much and greatly-needed alleviation to the sufferer.

Here, for the present, I must take leave of the 'Working Man's Memoirs,' as well as of his friendly and respected critics, in order that I may note some domestic incidents which, as I think, will serve to show that

> "There is a Providence that shapes our ends,
> Rough-hew them how we will."*

I had long been trying to establish a small book-selling and stationery business, with a view to procure a living for one of my younger sons. After much and earnest exertion, in which I was cheerfully seconded by my son, there seemed to be a fair prospect of our being enabled to realize our wishes. Suddenly, however, the prospect became

* I know not where to look for this quotation; but if it be in one of Shakspeare's plays, which I think it is, I cannot verify it, as I do not possess his works, nor are they readily within my reach. The reader will therefore pardon me if I have made any mistake. There is, however, in another book, a passage which will better suit my purpose, while I have no uncertainty as to the source from which it is derived:—"A man's heart deviseth his way, but the Lord directeth his steps." Concerning the truth of this declaration I can have no doubt, as in many and sometimes remarkable instances my purposes have been altogether and involuntarily changed, while the issue has been such as to convince me that a higher power than my own was employed therein.

overclouded: some of our best customers removed to distant neighbourhoods, while others declined to take any periodical publications after those with which we had served them were completed. Besides these we lost other customers, because they could then buy both books and stationery at a much cheaper rate than that at which we could afford to sell them. Thus, as we were cut off from all hope of being able to do any further good at bookselling, we resolved to give up that business altogether, and thenceforth to confine our attention wholly to tailoring; and, indeed, there now seemed good reason to hope that this occupation might become adequate to our wants. But this hope, like that previously indulged, soon vanished, for in the course of a few months we were left without anything like a sufficient amount of business. This adverse change was brought about by several causes, of which the chief were—the removal from our neighbourhood of several families who for some years had supplied us with a good deal of work, the decease of some of our customers, and the preference given by others to the professedly cheap tailors. In this dilemma, which was not a little perplexing, we were most unexpectedly cheered by an incident which seemed to warrant the hope that, after all our reverses and disappointments, we should not be left without the means of subsistence. This very seasonable encouragement came from a benevolent clergyman of the Established Church, to whom I had the pleasure of becoming known so far back as the year 1835. This gentleman had for some time been desirous of doing something on my behalf, and now resolved to use his influence towards getting one of my sons admitted into an institution where young men are prepared for the office of schoolmaster. When he told me of his generous purpose I was relieved of much anxiety, as I had been very much concerned about the future lot of him for whom my kind friend proposed to use his influence. I was not unaware that there were difficulties in the way of effecting his intention, but I was willing to believe that these would be surmounted. I advised my son to set about preparing himself for the examination which he would have to undergo, promising him all the assistance that I might be able to give him. Thus advised and encouraged, he forthwith went to work, while we jointly hoped for a good issue to the efforts we were making. To insure ourselves from interruption, we usually devoted the early morning hours to this business, and thus were enabled to get on with much better effect than otherwise would have been practicable.

At the end of a month from this time my pupil had made considerable improvement in several branches of elementary learning. In due time he was examined as to his attainments in these and other subjects, when, having acquitted himself satisfactorily, he was admitted into the institution.

His leaving home for a continuance was an event which was likely to have a somewhat depressing influence upon my feelings. For a long time he had been my chief companion; not, however, from any favouritism on my part (for I have at all times carefully avoided being governed or moved by that very mischievous feeling), but because he was necessarily much employed in a way which made it needful that he should have my ready superintendence. In order to compensate, so far as I could, for the loss of my companion, I had recourse to several expedients, of which I may perhaps hereafter give some account. It may, however, be well to name one of them now. This was to commit to paper any thoughts that might seem likely to be useful to young persons at the time when they finally leave the shelter of the parental roof. These thoughts may, possibly, at a future day find their way into print; for the present, however, they must keep company with the rather large assemblage of recorded but unpublished reflections which, in the course of the last thirty years, I have contrived to bring together. I conclude these notices of my recent domestic history by observing that I am, by means of the incidents recorded, more than ever satisfied concerning the truthfulness of what is affirmed in the preceding note.

I must now go on with what I have further to say to my generous critics. Of these there is no one that deserves a more particular and respectful notice than does the writer of the remarks upon the 'Memoirs,' in that justly popular publication 'The Edinburgh Journal.' This gentleman gives me credit for having written the 'Memoirs' in a style which, although "plain" and "homely," is yet "good English." So long as it possesses the last-named quality I am satisfied; for I not only carefully avoid all attempts at writing in an ornate style, as being unseemly in a man of my humble pretensions to literary talent, but also endeavour to write in language that shall be easily intelligible to the young and the untaught. If in *thus* writing I do not greatly violate grammatical rules, or fall into a coarse or rude mode of expressing my thoughts and feelings, I have gained all that I have either wished for or aimed at in this regard.

The reviewer goes on to express his regret that I should have been wholly silent as to both my " own name" and that of my "native town." He thinks that my silence was prompted by an "unnecessary delicacy," such as "deprives the reader of a main source of interest." On this I remark, that my concealment of these names was advisedly done. I considered that the objects aimed at in my little book were such as had no relation to either personal vanity or to the gratification of an idle, and perhaps also an ill-natured curiosity. I wrote neither for personal fame nor for the amusement of the merely inquisitive or frivolous reader. With regard to the former motive, I was then as I still am, and probably ever shall be, much of Dr. Franklin's opinion, that "solid pudding is better than empty praise;" while, as regards the satisfying the curiosity of a trifler, I was in no wise disposed to do so; but rather to answer his inquiries as to my name and birth-place, by simply replying,—

"My name, my country, what are they to thee?"

I believed that if any of my readers wished to befriend me, they would have no difficulty in discovering either my name or my dwelling-place; and that those who might merely wish to know who, or what, or where the author might be, without any intention of helping him, would not be likely to take much, if any trouble, even in the way of gratifying their own curiosity, and therefore would not be so likely to cause me pain by the ill-meant or captious remarks in which, otherwise, they would probably indulge. The issue proved that I judged rightly, for in several instances the readers of the book took the trouble to inquire about its author, in order that they might give him some substantial proof of their approbation of his work and of their goodwill towards himself. I am not at liberty to give the names of these generous persons, or I should be proud to record them here, in token of the gratitude which I feel for their spontaneous and encouraging kindness. As, however, the reviewer has so strongly expressed his wish that I had been more communicative in regard to my name and birth-place, I shall give some information concerning both. But I still wish to wear something of a mask, though it be only a partial one and worn loosely, and shall therefore adopt such a mode of expressing myself as will give the reader a little, but only a little (and, it may be, not unpleasant) trouble to interpret.

CHAPTER II.

As regards my "own name," I may remark that it is one which belongs to a very humble, yet ancient, if not primitive, occupation. It is derived from that of a vehicle which came into use very soon after our "rude forefathers" began to apply themselves to the cultivation of the ground and to the exchange of commodities. Both the vehicle and the occupation named therefrom soon became very generally known and used, and therefore when *surnames* were adopted, which names were in many instances drawn from the occupations of those who adopted them, it was quite natural that the name in question should not only come into use, but also become very common. It is still, as might be expected, a somewhat common name; so common, indeed, and moreover bespeaking so humble an origin, that several families, feeling (as it would seem) a little scandalized thereat, have ventured to alter its orthography by adding one or more letters, so as to conceal in some degree the fact of their having sprung from such an ignoble stock; yet after all their care and trouble, the original appellation may be recognized.

But, passing by this perhaps pardonable

weakness, I now come to indicate the name of my "native town."* If I am rightly instructed as regards its derivation, it is made up of two distinct words—the latter being the old word for "city," the former the name of an ancient British prince, concerning whom it has been long said, or sung, that he " was a merry old soul." The town is large and populous. It is a borough returning two members to Parliament. There are, in all, sixteen parishes included within its jurisdiction; but four of this number are chiefly of a rural character, consisting principally of fields and other cultivated grounds. They are situated, respectively, upon the four sides or extremities of the town, corresponding to the four cardinal points of the compass. In the twelve parishes which constitute what is properly the town, there are many objects calculated to interest an observant and intelligent spectator. Of these, one of the chief is an ancient castle, which I have often contemplated with much sober thoughtfulness and feeling. Although now much dilapidated, it still exhibits a fair specimen of this description of ancient architecture. It has yet remaining several spacious apartments in a tolerably

* Its history has been written by two, if not more, competent men: first by the Rev. Philip Morant, who wrote about the middle of the last century; and, secondly, in the early part of the current century by Mr. Cromwell, a descendant of the Protector.

complete state, one of which is used as a public library (among whose contents are many valuable books), while another is a depository for the arms and accoutrements of the militia regiment belonging to the district. There is also a room which was once used as a chapel, and where, when I last visited it, " the big ha' Bible " still kept its place upon the antique reading-desk. In the north-western corner of the castle-yard is a stone that marks the spot where fell two eminent men, by a military sentence, for the part which they had taken in the defence of the town while it was besieged by the Parliamentary army, in the Civil Wars of the seventeenth century. In the south-western angle of the castle there is a modern addition, in the shape of a low dome-covered tower, near which is (or at least *was*, when I was last there) a young and vigorous oak-tree. I have sometimes been curious to know whence it would derive a due supply of support and nourishment, in case it should continue to occupy its present out-of-the-way position.

But I must close my notice of this interesting relic of a long-departed age, and pass on to the ruins of what was once a large and magnificent church, dedicated to St. Botolph, and belonging to an adjacent priory, of which, however, there *now* remains no trace. These noble remains offer, even to the ordinary spectator, a very striking and pleasing object; while, to the well-instructed lover of ancient ecclesiastical architecture, they are of much higher and more enduring interest, exhibiting, as they do, a fine specimen of ancient art. This is especially the case in regard to the western front, a gateway (or rather a porch) in which is allowed to be a very finished and beautiful piece of workmanship. There was formerly an unsightly excrescence upon the top of this front, consisting of some modern brickwork, surmounted by a paltry-looking vane, but this, by the good taste of a late incumbent, was removed, so that now there is nothing of modern date to detract from the impressive beauty of these remains of a once glorious structure. The interior space is, indeed, partly filled by modern tombs, but these, as I venture to think, do not so much break in upon the antique and venerable character of the edifice as to destroy, or even greatly to injure, its general expression. On the contrary, they may seem, to a thoughtful and judicious observer, rather to harmonize with than to be opposed to the solemn, yet pleasing, emotions which these venerable time-worn relics are calculated to produce. Many a time have I felt the power of this or a similar object to awaken thoughts and feelings of a highly pleasing, although perchance a grave character. For more than seven years I saw this ruined pile almost daily, yet, whenever at liberty to look at it with attention, I felt that its power to affect either the fancy or the heart was in no degree changed or diminished. Thus, for example, whether it were illumed by the glorious light of the morning sun, or by the subdued splendour of his evening beams, or by the yet milder radiance of " Night's fair Queen," it often served to carry my thoughts back to long-departed years, and to present me with ideal pictures of its former aspect, when it stood forth " proudly eminent," as a specimen of what human art and industry can perform, especially when, as in this case, they are prompted by the powerful influence of strong religious feeling. Often too has it reminded me of the " assembled men" who, within its consecrated precincts, were accustomed to unite in the exercises of public worship, while in harmonious and spirit-stirring accompaniment with their " long-resounding" voices,—

"The pealing organ swell'd the note of praise."

And further, although I was aware that these services were conducted in strict accordance with the ritual of the Roman Catholic Church, and therefore attended by many ceremonies which are perhaps justly deemed to be unauthorised and of no genuine worth, I nevertheless could not but believe that many of the worshippers were of a sincerely devout and Christian-like character, and that (being so) they were, when they ceased to dwell on this earth, admitted "into the heavens," and made the happy companions and the fellow-worshippers of "the spirits of just men made perfect."

Such were some of the thoughts and feelings of which I was then sometimes the subject, by means of contemplating these jointly impressive and suggestive ruins. I have noted them thus minutely, for the purpose of showing the way by which an object which in general is regarded as being one of mere curiosity, may be made to subserve a far higher and more enduring purpose than that of pleasing the eye or amusing a vagrant fancy.

Having dwelt so long upon this particular object, I must be the more brief concerning many others, which, as I believe, deserve to be noticed. Among these are several other ancient churches, four of which were formerly in a ruinous state, but subsequently were so far restored as to make them available for public service. The modern works, however, are in great part rather incongruous additions to those upon which they have been grafted, showing very plain marks of either the poverty, the tastelessness, or the religious indifference of the times when they were erected. Another church which, with the exception of a part of its tower, was destroyed during the siege already mentioned, has been rebuilt. It is a neat and commodious structure, but has nothing about it that calls for any special remark. The burial-ground attached to this church is spacious, and being intersected by broad footpaths, which are bordered and overshadowed by large trees, affords a not unpleasing walking-place, especially to those who are not unwilling to be reminded of man's frailty and inevitable mortality. It is crowded with tombs and turf-covered graves, among which I frequently when a child threaded my way, for the purpose of amusement, as here I could in their season find king-cups and daisies, while sometimes I captured a butterfly, or found entertainment in watching the operations of the industrious rooks, whose homes were upon the trees, or of the less thrifty daws, which had found their dwelling-places in the " nooks and corners" of the " ivy-mantled tower." But even at that early age I was not wholly insensible to the solemnity of this " place of graves." Often have I observed, with much of serious and awe-stricken feeling, the many fragments of coffins or of partly decomposed human remains, which were brought to view by the sexton, while preparing a receptacle for the tenantless and already decaying body of one recently departed. In subsequent years I have often beheld the same, but then aged and almost decrepit man, wielding mattock or shovel, in performing the same office for such as, although " by far his juniors," had been removed from the much-loved gaieties or the irksome anxieties of this life.

Here, too, in years comparatively recent, have I frequently walked, " with faltering step and slow," and while I contemplated the graves around me, could not but think that the strangely disordered and much shattered state of my earthly " tabernacle" was an almost certain intimation that ere long I also should be called hence, to

> "That undiscover'd country, from whose bourne
> No traveller returns."

Since then, however, more than as many years as were added to the life of the ancient Jewish monarch have passed away, and I am still among the living, and taking, so far as I am enabled to do, my allotted part in the various duties and relations of this probationary state of being. But I must drop these reflections, and resume my story.

The western side of this " burying-place " is bounded by the town wall, through a breach in which there is a descending outlet into the adjacent public way. The wall is of great thickness, and of so closely compacted and firm a substance as to seem to be almost indestructible; yet, although in this part it is in a tolerably perfect state, in some others it is a mere wreck; while, in not a few places, it has been totally broken down. Its whole course can, however, be easily traced, as the points at which the gates of the town formerly stood, still bear their distinctive appellations, and thus serve as way-marks to the inquirer. The river, which passes by the town, runs near the northern side of the wall, and here, in one of the breaches, I have sometimes amused myself by trying to detach some fragment of stone or brick from the cement which fastened it to the mass. My efforts were, however, almost invariably unsuccessful; so firmly were the several materials united, that no exertion which I could make was equal to the labour of breaking off even the smallest portion. I could not but observe the great dissimilarity between this ancient work and the generality of modern structures, in regard to the qualities of adhesiveness and durability.

When a boy, and before I was troubled by asthma, I often indulged myself in the cleanly and healthful habit of bathing, the public place for which was a part of the river near the spot of which I have just been writing. On one of these occasions I saw two birds (of beautiful form and colour) which had perched upon a rail that projected into the stream. Having but little knowledge of ornithology I was at a loss to determine either what they were or from whence they came; nor could I get any information upon these points for some considerable time, when I learned that they must have been specimens of the bird called the "king-fisher."

Near to this spot also, on a lovely summer morning, I witnessed a very sad spectacle; this was the lifeless body of a young man—a military officer

—who had, just before, fallen a victim to that mistaken notion of honour, once so prevalent among the higher classes of society. A foolish squabble at the mess-table on the preceding evening gave occasion for this appeal to arms, which terminated fatally to one of the parties concerned, and involved the others in much immediate trouble; and, moreover, if they were men capable of right feeling, must in after-life have given rise to many a bitter but unavailing pang of remorse. Not very far from hence I also once beheld another mournful sight, in the person of an aged man, who, in the ordinary course of nature, death must soon have relieved of all his earthly afflictions and privations, but who, in order to escape from them still earlier, had precipitated himself into the river. In this instance I saw what I felt to be an affecting and admonitory example of the miserable state of man, when he has no " hope towards God," and consequently no support for his spirit in the " day of adversity."

Here I am reminded, that in this vicinity, about which I have already said so much, there lived a man and his wife, part of whose history I think to be instructive, and therefore worthy of notice. When I was a child they kept a respectable public-house, and were respected for their civility, good order, and upright dealing. In an evil hour, as it proved to be for them, they came into possession of several hundred pounds, by means of what was called a "lucky" speculation in the state lottery, that once fruitful source of wide-spread misery, and crime. This sudden acquisition of what was to them great wealth produced a total change in their habits and characters; they became negligent of their business, grossly intemperate, and ruinously improvident. In a comparatively short time they got rid not only of their new and easily acquired property, but also of all that they possessed besides, and for which they had laboured diligently for many a year. Insolvency and ruin came upon them, and they had to begin the world anew, and moreover in very humble occupations; here, however, their former good habits returned, and in due time they again became and continued to be respected, both for their becoming demeanour and their diligent attention to business. I never observed anything like discontent on the part of either of them; on the contrary, I have rarely witnessed more cheerfulness and evident contentment in connection with a really humble station.

I now waive further digression, in order that I may give some account of the four outlying parishes to which I have already alluded. That which lies on the western extremity of the town is, as I think, worthy of special remark, on account of its many picturesque scenes and objects, which from my earliest recollection have made it to me a very delightful locality. Its neat, if not elegant,

c

church is its chief architectural ornament;* while the old manor-house is not without its interest, serving as it does to remind the spectator of the people and the manners of a bygone age. In the gardens of this antiquated mansion I have, by the favour of a friend, sometimes spent a pleasant hour; they could indeed boast little beauty, being a good deal of that formal character in which

"Grove nods to grove, each alley has its brother,
And half the landscape just reflects the other;"

yet they afforded a welcome retreat to one who, wearied by the bustle and turmoil of the busy town, needed the refreshing influence of quiet and retirement.

In the vicinity of the village there are the remains of embankments and trenches, that were

"the ramparts once
Of iron war, in ancient barbarous times,
When disunited Britain ever bled."

---

* This is of modern date, and I presume not to find any fault with it; yet I prefer the old one, because of its having been not only more in accordance with the homeliness of a rustic village, but also because of its being associated in my imagination with the years of my childhood and early youth. The old structure recurs to my memory whenever I think of

"The decent church which topp'd the neighb'ring hill,"

and which forms so prominent and not less beautiful a feature in Goldsmith's graphic description of a country village.

In my childhood there was for several months a military encampment upon the adjoining heath, and then these ancient works were, in many places, chosen by the sutlers and other usual followers of an army as the sites of their temporary habitations. If there be truth in what has been affirmed as to the genuine beauty of objects which although "often seen" still continue to give pleasure, it follows that many in and about this village and its neighbourhood have a legitimate claim to be considered as beautiful. I judge thus because I always find pleasure in contemplating them, whether or not they recall images or reflections of any incident or fact in which I either have been or am personally interested.

I now turn to take a glance at the parish which lies on the southern side of the town; this has no village, nor does it contain any object worthy of particular regard, except its church,—an edifice of small size and humble aspect, although perchance it was reared by one who was not unskilled in his art, as it is said to have, even in its present decayed and defaced condition, some features which deserve the approbation of the critic in ancient ecclesiastical architecture. It is, unless a change has recently been made, half-embosomed among some aged trees; and is further thrown into the shade by a plantation of lofty firs, through which a winding footpath leads from the adjacent manor-house into the churchyard, which is one of the most quiet and otherwise attractive places of the kind that I have ever seen.

In this sequestered and hallowed spot the meditative mind may, without interruption, carry on its musings, and, forgetting the lapse of time, may

"Think down hours to moments."

I have ever felt that the scene which it presents invites to such thoughts and feelings as may, for the time, seem to carry the spirit far away from the earth and its shadows into the regions of genuine and unfading blessedness. It had perhaps been impossible that I should have contemplated this, to me, very suggestive scene, without calling to mind that beautiful stanza in Gray's unequalled 'Elegy:'—

"Hark! how the sacred calm that breathes around
　Bids ev'ry fierce tumultuous passion cease;
In still, small accents, whisp'ring from the ground
　The grateful earnest of eternal peace."

While musing on these beautifully expressive and touching lines* I have almost seemed to hear these gentle whisperings, issuing alike from the turf-crowned grave of the peasant, and from the more costly monument raised over the mortal remains

* It may be proper to observe that this stanza does not appear in the 'Elegy' as usually printed. It is one out of four stanzas which formed part of the first MS. of the poem, but which were subsequently struck out.

of his former master. These soft yet eloquent breathings have appeared to give an assurance, or at least a cheering intimation, that, in like manner as the once over-tasked and toil-worn bodily frame was resting from all its labours—so, the " freed spirit," erewhile harassed by cares or depressed by affliction, had found a safe and quiet resting-place; from which no inhabitant ever departs, and into which neither danger nor trouble shall ever be permitted to intrude.

These would be delightful truths, even if it were less certain than it is that they are founded on the basis of genuine truth. That they *are* thus founded will, perhaps, appear to be more than merely probable to all who listen to the dictates of right reason and of divine revelation. These will not find it difficult to believe, that, amidst much of ignorance or of involuntary error, there may be sincerity of heart, and therefore that many an untaught peasant is a spiritual worshipper and servant of the true God, and thus is being prepared for a place in the heavenly temple.

In this rustic graveyard there are but few monuments of a costlier description than the turf-covered hillock; and these are, of course, unlikely to attract particular attention. Among those, however, of a higher order there is (or was at the time referred to) one which, although untouched by the corroding hand of time, and free from all marks of human defacement, bears no traces of an inscription. This unusual omission, in the case of a "monumental stone," must have been wholly inexplicable to many who have noticed it; but to those who are acquainted with the history of him the resting-place of whose mortal relics it points out, this uninscribed and unadorned head-stone tells a tale at once deeply pathetic and replete with solemn admonition. It is a memorial of one who, in the "wild chase" of pleasure, had drained the cup of sensual delight to its veriest dregs long before he had reached the noontide of life, and then, in an evil hour—an hour of bitter anguish and of "desperate sorrow"—was induced

"Against his own sad breast to lift the hand
Of impious violence."*

In one of the humbler graves were deposited many years ago the remains of my paternal grandfather, of whom I have heard my mother speak in the language of respect and commendation; and who would seem to have been an industrious, sober, and otherwise worthy man. Late in life he followed his children, who had migrated from their

* By a compromise, as it would seem, between the then existing law regarding suicide and the benevolent feelings prompted by Christian principles, his body was allowed to be deposited within the pale of this consecrated enclosure, but not to have its place of sepulture more plainly marked out than by an uninscribed stone.

native village and had settled in this parish. Here he dwelt until, in a good old age, he was called, as I would hope, to a higher and a happier state of being.

The pathway from the church to the town leads through some fields, which, however, present no features of sufficient interest to call for any particular notice; yet, even here, I have sometimes derived entertainment from objects which were, in all conscience, simple enough, and without even the merit of being uncommon. But it is perhaps not altogether unwise to allow oneself to be sometimes pleased even with " trifles light as air." On these occasions the object of my amusement was a multitudinous assemblage of wild rabbits, which were congregated with a view, as I judged, both to recreation and refection. I hardly need say that rabbits are very lively and frolicsome animals; or that they are active and adventurous in their search after food. One of these fields was the scene also of some of my childish amusements. The greater part of its area is a large and deep pit, from which sand and gravel were formerly taken, but which has for many years been covered with greensward. Down the sides of this hollow I have both run and rolled, when, for the time, I felt something of the gladsomeness of heart which belongs to the season of early childhood, and which, in many instances, is powerfully influential in deadening the sense of bodily pain or infirmity.

Here also I made my first attempt at riding, not indeed on horseback, but on the back of an ass— that much-despised and often harshly-treated beast, whose good qualities, however, very far outnumber its faults, justly entitling it to all that kind-hearted consideration which the worthy Sancho Panza is said to have bestowed upon his deserving and esteemed "Dapple." I was, however, far enough from being successful in this somewhat bold experiment, for as soon as my donkey began to move rather briskly I was unseated and brought to the ground, thus giving but small intimation that I should ever

"Witch the world with noble horsemanship."

Between this field and the town there is an open piece of ground, commonly called "the Green," but whose full and proper name includes that of an eminent apostle of Christianity, to whom was dedicated an abbey which formerly stood hard by, but which has long been in ruins, and almost entirely

"Buried midst the wreck of things which were!"

The only remaining trace of this once extensive establishment is a quadrangular and pinnacled tower, through which was the principal entrance to the abbey—with perhaps some parts of a wall enclosing the grounds that formed the abbey gardens. These have long been held by a market-gardener, whose house is in part composed of the tower. When a child, he was placed under my good mother's care, and this led to my having some pleasant walks in these grounds, as well as some welcome treats in the shape of fruit.

I will now briefly notice the two out-parishes which respectively skirt the eastern and northern sides of the town. Of that on the eastern side I know but little that is remarkable. Its church is, I believe, an ancient structure, but I am not aware that it contains anything very interesting, either in its architectural features, or in its monuments: it stands upon an eminence from which there is a pleasing view of the eastern and north-eastern quarters of the town, with their respective suburbs. The northerly situated parish deserves a little longer notice, inasmuch as in several places it affords an extensive and picturesque view of the town; from some points, indeed, I think the prospect may fairly be called beautiful. The church is a lowly-looking rustic edifice of small size, yet sufficiently large for its required purposes. The parsonage-house is of modern date, and of a somewhat elegant aspect, especially when contrasted with the closely adjacent church. The ground hereabouts is considerably elevated, but gradually declines until it nearly reaches the river, from the opposite bank of which there is a gradual ascent; on the upper part and the summit of which the greater part of the town is situated, and presents, from the point just referred to, a varied and not uninteresting prospect.

Within the limits of this parish there are woodlands, fields, and meadows, where in my earlier years I enjoyed many a pleasant ramble, and passed many a quiet and delightful hour, sometimes with a companion, but in general alone; yet, even then, I felt nothing of lonesomeness, for I had learned to hold converse with scenes and objects such as were then present. While thus engaged, I was not seldom led to think of Him to whom every object owes its existence, with all that it possesses of either sublimity or beauty. Perhaps I may be permitted to observe that, if natural objects be not merely the faint resemblances or mementos of spiritual realities, but their genuine and proper representatives, it would seem to follow that the study of nature's volume may be made fully as ameliorating to the moral feelings, as it is enlightening to the intellect and entertaining to the imagination. But I may not enlarge upon this topic, interesting and important though it be, as my present business is not with abstruse questions, but with simple facts or incidents. Nor ought I, perhaps, further to pursue the account of my rambles, and of their influence upon my feelings; yet it may be well to notice that the remembrance of scenes and objects with which we were entertained in our earlier or healthier years may be made, as I know by much personal experience, sources of true pleasure in seasons of bodily illness, or amidst the manifold infirmities that usually accompany our declining years. It is in this way that we can, as it were,

"———————————— reimport
The period past ——————"

and a second time enjoy the recreations or the higher pleasures in which the heart may legitimately, perhaps laudably, feel an earnest and an abiding interest. The young and the healthy would do well to reflect that their present vigour and activity may soon be lost, or if not, that "old age comes on apace," bringing with it physical weakness, and perhaps other causes of uneasiness or despondency. In either case they will need all the alleviations that may be within their reach; but, as external appliances are of little efficacy unless the heart is at rest, let it be their present and only great concern to see that the understanding be well instructed, the affections duly regulated, and the memory largely stored. Thus they will be prepared for the time when, for want of these needful preparatives, multitudes of their species are destitute of all internal quietude, and consequently of all true support—exhibiting humiliating spectacles of unalleviated wretchedness.

Wishing that these hints may be as well received as they are earnestly given, I now take leave of my critic, as also of the 'Edinburgh Journal,' and proceed to address a few words to the gentleman who wrote the remarks upon my little book, which were published in the 'Churchman's Monthly Review' for March, 1845.

Here, however, I am somewhat at a loss what to say. I am not disposed to be querulous, yet I cannot help thinking that I have some reason to complain. Waiving, however, all merely personal feelings, I come directly to the point at issue, and must express my regret that a Christian gentleman — and moreover a clergyman — should have allowed himself to violate the strict rule of right, while engaged in his critical duties. I refer to his having adopted the very unfair and disreputable practice of giving a positive and final judgment upon books without having read them; or, at best, after having given them only a partial and careless perusal. I will not permit myself even so much as to suspect this gentleman of having done me wilful and intentional wrong; but that he has committed the fault of giving an unwarranted and one-sided decision is, I think, beyond all question. For example, he has raised a great, and what is evidently meant to be a damaging objection to the 'Memoirs,' upon a mere fragment of a somewhat long paragraph. From this scrap, considered apart from the context, and interpreted according to the opinions, or rather the prejudices, of the reviewer, it is made to appear that the "working-man" is greatly indifferent as to the character or tendency of what are affirmed to be religious principles—so indifferent, indeed, as to deserve the name of a "latitudinarian." Such an inference as this, however, is not fairly deducible from the author's words; and yet this critic, forgetting at the time what was due to his own character and station, no less than what is inculcated by Christian charity, deliberately sets down the working-man as one holding very loose, if not, indeed, heretical notions. He, therefore, takes a good deal of what is in truth very unnecessary trouble, in order to guard the readers of the 'Memoirs,' who he thinks will be rather numerous, against what he considers to be the dangerous tendency of the passage in question.*

* That the reader may readily be able to see the grounds upon which the charge of latitudinarianism is made to rest, the passage of the 'Memoirs' referred to in the text is here given:—" As to myself, I am not careful about either standards of doctrine, or modes of worship, or rules of discipline. To whichsoever of these diverse matters any one may give the preference is to me quite indifferent; all I wish for is to see a practical attention to the duties which the Christian religion enjoins, and a fair amount of resemblance, in regard to Christian charity, between the professed disciple and his beneficent Master." The paragraph, of which this passage forms but a small part, may be found at pages 129 and 130 of the 'Memoirs.'

After this objection, founded upon a mere assumption, the reviewer goes on to another very brief passage, from which also he draws conclusions impugning the orthodoxy of the author. In this passage allusion is made to some sermons written by an "eminent Unitarian minister," who unquestionably was a learned and very amiable man. Because this gentleman and his sermons are noticed in terms of what were thought to be those of only becoming respect, the reviewer again violates the divine law of Christian charity, and forthwith proceeds to condemn the author. Further on he has, with mingled bad taste and ill-temper, allowed himself to apply what he perhaps meant to be disparaging epithets to the "working-man," calling him a "literary adventurer," and Mr. Knight's "workman," closing his remarks by an expression of pity for the author, on account of his assumed dereliction of orthodox religious principles. To all this a very few words will suffice for an answer. The "working-man" continues to aim at earning a living by following his proper business, that of a tailor; he does this, moreover, to the utmost of his power and opportunity. There are few working days in which, if at all able, he does not spend more hours at this occupation than his uncandid and uncharitable critic would perhaps feel to be quite consistent with his own health or comfort. The fact of the "working-man" being usually thus employed is distinctly noted at page 233 of the 'Memoirs.'

Before taking leave of this gentleman I will just intimate that I believe him to be one to whom I am personally known. If this conjecture be correct, I am indebted to him for some acts of kindness which, more than twenty years ago, he performed on my behalf, in return for my having done what I felt to be an imperative duty. If he and the reviewer be the same person, I then have to observe that I have not ceased, nor shall I cease, to be grateful to the patron, although I have ventured to censure the critic.

I now turn to the gentleman who reviewed the 'Memoirs' in the 'Critic' of August 2, 1845. I am bound to give expression to my grateful feelings on account of the kindly and liberal spirit in which that review is written. In general, the reviewer has rightly interpreted such parts of the 'Memoirs' as in his opinion needed it. His conjecture, that " the book was written with a strong practical design," is perfectly just. It was truly my intention to make such a book as might tend to realize the sentiment implied by the line which I chose as my motto—

"If I one soul improve I have not lived in vain."

This gentleman will, I believe, be glad to learn that I have received from more than a few quarters the very encouraging assurance, that my attempt to be useful to others has not been wholly abortive. Thus I am doubly recompensed for my labour; as I have the cheering reflection that I have been in some degree instrumental in advancing the great work of intellectual and moral improvement, while the payment received for my manuscript has relieved me from pecuniary embarrassments to a much greater extent than I had ventured to hope.

It may seem ungracious on my part to find fault with this generous critic; yet there are one or two points upon which I cannot but wish that he had expressed a different opinion. Through the want of adequate information, he has fallen into an error, which I feel confident he would, if needful, willingly correct, and therefore I have no fear of giving him offence by adverting to it. He commends me, and I thank him for that commendation, for having maintained a proper silence in regard to my domestic affairs. But, although I have in general been cautious in this respect, I have not been quite so reserved upon one particular subject as the reviewer represents me to have been when he says, "Of the partner of his domestic joys we hear little or nothing." Now, although more than one weighty reason is assigned for my silence, yet, as I most earnestly desire to stand well in the estimation of my *female* readers, I could wish that what I have either hinted or plainly expressed concerning my conjugal partner had been more fully brought before the readers of the review; for although I was purposely very sparing of words upon this point, I yet gave more than a few intimations of the estimation in which I held both the character and the conduct of one who, through many a dark and dreary year of trouble and affliction, has proved to be all, nay, more than all, that I could fairly have expected. I must not, however, enlarge upon a subject like this; yet it may be allowable to observe, in passing, that I have found my partner what I fully believe every woman of plain good sense and right feelings to be—far more faithful to her engagements than can easily be expressed. Suffice it to say, that my now somewhat long experience of domestic life, although chequered by much of an afflictive and troublous character, has confirmed me in an opinion concerning women that I had formed long before I became a married man; I still firmly believe that the marriage state, with all its necessary and contingent anxieties, is very much to be preferred to a life of celibacy. I state this with an especial reference to people of my own class in society. From these avowals, then, it may easily be inferred what are my opinions and feelings concerning not merely one woman, but the female sex in general. I will only add that I never have been a believer of the common stories about bad wives, but have ever held, as I now hold, that no woman is a bad wife unless she be married to a man who is not a truly good husband.

But I must now pass on to another part of the review, in which there is a mistake as to my religious profession, or rather as to the particular section of the Christian Church to which I belong. The reviewer is unable to account for the working-man's " warm and almost poetical sympathy with, and admiration of, the services, the rites, and the temples of the Church of England," viewed in connection " with a steady adherence to the sect of dissenters to which his family had belonged." He goes on to say that the working-man " has a keen sense of the beauties of Gothic architecture, and even a reverence for the persons of the English clergy; and yet, in spite of this, he cleaves to a congregation, the very first principle of fellowship with which is the belief that the ceremonies of the church are superstitious and dangerous in their tendencies." To all this I have to say that there is nothing in the 'Memoirs' to warrant the conclusion that I continued to be a dissenter from the Church of England. In this instance, therefore, my respected critic has assumed the premises of his argument, and from thence has jumped to a conclusion. The fact is, that I have not belonged to, nor in any way been associated with, the religious body to which I once belonged, for more than twenty years, as I seceded from it in the year 1828, when I became a member of that large class of separatists from the Church of England which is not numbered among the dissenters, inasmuch as it retains the use of the Church liturgy, and inculcates feelings of respect for the entire Church establishment. Of late years, however, I have not been in fact a member of either this or any other Christian community; as my increasing, and to strangers troublesome infirmities, have prevented my attendance upon public worship. Thus I have silently, and without intending it, ceased to be acknowledged by any sect or denomination of Christians. Meanwhile I have been neither indifferent nor thoughtless in regard to ecclesiastical matters; on the contrary, I have observed (according to my opportunity and ability) the course of action followed by the different religious communities; and I have also thought soberly, and I believe candidly, upon their several claims to the approbation of either the public at large or of private individuals; and the result has been that I have come to regard the Church of England as having a just and strong claim upon the genuine respect and the cordial sympathies of the whole English people.

There is a third mistake into which the reviewer has fallen, which, however, might have been easily avoided. I much regret that this mistake has been made—first, because of the necessity which it imposes upon me to complain of a gentleman for whom I cannot but feel a high degree of respect; and secondly, because its tendency is to give the reader of the 'Memoirs' a widely erroneous notion of their author's religious principles and feelings. The passage in which this mistake occurs is as follows: "One defect of his mind, originating in a bad state of society, is the absence of strong distinctive religious feeling; in calamity his main support is in a philosophical, not a religious resignation. This is connected in all probability with the fact that no mention is made of any minister of religion as interesting himself in the spiritual or temporal well-being of the working-man. This is bad: the poor man who is to be rendered better and wiser by books of this nature ought to have his thoughts more frequently directed to Him who careth for the poor."

On this passage I must remark that I am unable to determine whether or not I rightly understand what is meant by the phrase "strong distinctive religious feeling." I suppose, however, that the emphasis is intended to be placed upon the word "distinctive," as I can hardly believe that the reviewer could intend to represent the writer of the 'Memoirs' as being destitute of even a "strong" religious feeling; since he was far too explicit upon this point to be easily misunderstood. I therefore confine my remarks to the word "distinctive."

If by this term be meant that exclusive attachment to the doctrines, the discipline, or the ritual of any one section of the Christian Church, which either prompts or allows feelings of hostility (or even so much as of dislike) towards the members of other sections of that Church, I freely confess that I neither have nor wish to have any such feelings; on the contrary, if I had the least suspicion that they would come upon me, I should, as a matter of strict duty, endeavour to be on my guard against them; and for this reason, viz. that I am constrained to regard them as being, not only inconsistent with true Christian charity, but also as having in them the very essence of a deadly sin. Nothing (as I believe) can justify, if indeed it can palliate, the violation of the divine law of Christian love. So paramount are the claims of this law, that not even the most sincere and zealous regard for truth can ever compensate for the neglect of the duties which it enjoins. When, moreover, it is considered that even the most pious and intelligent of human beings has no claim to infallibility, and therefore cannot be quite sure that all which he believes, and believes, it may be, most firmly, is in strict agreement with genuine truth, it will readily be seen that no one is justified in severely and definitively judging (or even censuring) another, since it is more than possible that even the most acute and discriminating mind may err in its conclusions, and thus be led to give an opinion of others totally at variance with both equity and charity.

On these and other accounts I am not anxious to be remarkable for a "strong distinctive" feeling in relation to religious communities and modes of worship. The reviewer must bear with the seeming latitudinarianism of the working-man, for, after all, it is only in appearance that he is lax in respect of any religious principles, but especially such as are plainly of a fundamental character.

Further, it should be borne in mind that there is something very suspicious about that show of an exclusive preference for newly adopted forms or opinions, which is so frequently, and sometimes so very offensively, made by recent proselytes, and which therefore ought to be carefully avoided. When, moreover, it is remembered that the working-man was brought up among some of the strictest dissenters from the Church of England, and that he is now, from a sober conviction of its just merits, friendly to episcopacy, it may perhaps be allowed to him to cherish feelings of good-will towards such as are not within the pale of the Established Church, without being set down as culpable for not having a "strong distinctive religious feeling."

As to the assertion, that "in calamity his main support is in a philosophical, not a religious resignation," I cannot understand how any one who had fairly read the 'Memoirs' should have come to a conclusion, not only so far wide of the truth, but moreover so entirely at variance with many of the author's direct statements or plain intimations. It is, indeed, quite true that I have repeatedly expressed myself in terms which, taken by themselves and judged rigidly, might seem to warrant the opinion that I have sometimes consented to be quiet under the pressure of adverse circumstances merely because I saw it would be useless to be otherwise, thus making a virtue of what was a matter of only common prudence, if not of real necessity. But then there is a much greater number of instances in which I have plainly avowed my full and firm belief in the doctrine of a Divine Providence, both general and particular; and it is by these avowals that the true meaning of the phrases objected against ought to have been determined. As to the word "philosophical," I am not much in love with it; in general, it is used in a far too vague and accommodating way to allow of my employing it. When applied to morals I perceive that it may be made to mean almost anything, according to the predilections or the prejudices of those who use it. For myself, I freely avow that I have no faith in any moral philosophy that is not entirely built upon the broad foundations of natural and revealed truth, the first-named species of truth being, as far as is possible, investigated by means of the latter.

Amidst the multiplied and somewhat heavy troubles with which, for many years, I have had to contend, I had been but poorly supported or consoled, had my only, or even my chief resource, been that of the cheerless and to me very repulsive doctrine of necessity. I cannot in any degree receive this doctrine, although it be the main pillar upon which some systems of moral philosophy are made to rest. Nothing less than a firm and calm reliance upon the wisdom and the benevolence of Divine Providence could have either sustained the spirit or comforted the heart, when suffering under the double pressure of distressing bodily disorder and domestic anxieties. That I did not more frequently advert to these sources of consolation was a matter of set purpose. I did not intend to make the 'Memoirs' bear the aspect of what is called a "religious" book; and therefore I advisedly abstained from the frequent introduction of directly religious topics. I was led to adopt this plan by a wish not to give a repulsive air or character to a book which I wished to be read by those for whose welfare I felt concerned, but who, as I judged, would not be likely to read it if it dwelt much, or very plainly, upon the grave subjects connected with religion. Thus, I wrote what I thought to be of a religious tendency, rather than what was of an exclusively religious character. How far I have succeeded in accomplishing my purpose is not for me to say; but I may, and perhaps ought to state, that I have had the great satisfaction of receiving the encouraging testimony of many worthy and judicious persons as to the good moral tendency of my little book.

This testimony in conjunction with much of a similar kind, coming from among those who direct public opinion, served to confirm me in my views as to the propriety of my having endeavoured to write *that* which should aim at combining entertainment with instruction, rather than what, from its being altogether of a grave or didactic character, would probably have been neglected by those who read chiefly if not wholly for amusement.

Let these remarks suffice by way of answer to the charge of making what is called philosophy, rather than religion, the "main support" of the mind and heart in the day of trouble or of "calamity."

I must now notice what my respected critic has stated as to the degree in which I have been favoured with the oversight of Christian ministers. He affirms that in the 'Memoirs' "no mention is made of any minister of religion as interesting himself in the spiritual or temporal well-being of the working man." To this I shall perhaps best reply by quoting a passage which, judging from what the reviewer has said in another place, I might

D

fairly infer he had read; although it would seem to have subsequently escaped his remembrance. In this passage, I remarked, in reference to the clergy of the Established Church, "I cannot adequately express the sense I have of the courtesy, the urbanity, and the genuine kindness with which I have been treated by not a few of these excellent men and accomplished gentlemen."* I cannot allow myself to think that the reviewer intentionally omitted to notice this very explicit declaration concerning the obligations under which I have been placed by "not a few" of the ministers of the church to which, I presume, he belongs. I therefore can only account for the omission by supposing that he did not remember it, when he made the above-quoted remark, to which remark I offer the following answer:—

When writing the 'Memoirs' I was careful not to be more communicative upon several subjects, including this, than I thought to be needful or prudent. Now, however, (as it appears I am called upon to do so,) I will state freely why it is that I so much venerate many of the Episcopal clergy. I am not at liberty to be so explicit on this matter as my feelings prompt me to be, but I will use no reserve except where to do so is plainly my duty. In the foremost rank of these justly honoured patrons, I must place one whom I cannot but con-

* See p. 129 of the 'Memoirs.'

sider to be the most perfect specimen of the Christian gentleman that I have ever seen. This truly exemplary man has not only visited me in the time of sickness, but has often cheered me by his seasonable and Christian-like sympathy in other times of adversity. In addition to these favours, I was allowed ready access to him, whenever I wished to have the aid of his judicious counsel, or of his countenance in any of my humble yet sometimes perplexing affairs. I have not had the high pleasure of seeing him during the last sixteen or seventeen years, but I have retained a place in his remembrance, and not unfrequently have been favoured with his encouraging epistolary communications. To say that I regard this true gentleman and eminent Christian minister with feelings of gratitude and veneration is saying but little towards conveying even a moderately adequate idea of the deep sense which I have of his worth, on the one hand, and of my obligations to him, on the other.

Of another Episcopal clergyman it were difficult for me to speak too highly, in regard to his great and unwearied kindness to myself and family during the last fourteen years. Although I have never resided within the limits of the district under his pastoral care, yet he has often exercised on my behalf some of the most important functions of a Christian minister. I take great pleasure in thus recording the kindness which has given him a just claim to all the gratitude and respect that I can possibly express, whether by word or deed.

There is yet a third minister of the Established Church to whom I desire to pay a tribute of more than ordinary respect. This gentleman has, on very many occasions, given me the benefit of his generous patronage and of his active sympathy, for which I cannot but regard him with the most unaffected and grateful veneration. I might easily multiply instances of Christian-like kindness and benevolence; but these, perhaps, may suffice to show that I am bound to speak in terms of more than mere "reverence" of the " English clergy;" many of whom have, indeed, such strong claims upon my respect and gratitude, that I should rejoice were I able to offer them some better acknowledgment than can be made by mere verbal assurances. I would fain hope that what I have here stated may serve to acquit these " ministers of religion" of the charge of having been careless as to either the " spiritual or the temporal well-being of the working man;" and, with the earnest expression of this hope, I now take a respectful leave of my friendly and, as I believe, kindhearted reviewer.

Here, perhaps, it would be well to dismiss both the 'Memoirs' and the critics, as I may become tedious to the reader if I continue to dwell upon them. There are, however, two notices of my little volume which I am unwilling to pass by without remark;

and the more so, because they come from writers whose native country lies on the northern side of the Tweed, for which country and its inhabitants I have long felt a particular regard. One of these notices is contained in Hogg's 'Weekly Instructor,' for September 27, 1845, and might well make me, as it assuredly did, " right glad of heart," inasmuch as it breathes a spirit of cordial good-will towards the working man; while it distinctly recognises the morally useful tendency of the 'Memoirs.'

The other article appeared in the 'Alloa Advertiser,' for December 6, 1845, a publication of a very respectable order, combining the features of a local newspaper with those of a literary journal. Of this notice also I am bound to speak in terms of unqualified approbation. The writer has, as indeed he richly deserves to have, my warmest thanks.*

* This gentleman, as I have reason to believe, is a clergyman of the Scottish Episcopalian Church, and is much and deservedly respected.

CHAPTER III.

I now come to matters in which the reader may perhaps feel a livelier interest than in what relates to reviews and reviewers. I must, however, premise that I have but little to relate which rises much above the ordinary character of every-day life. I question, indeed, whether my recent personal history has been so fruitful in regard to incidents as might be wished; but I will endeavour to make up this deficiency by what, I hope, will not be deemed wholly uninteresting.

Since the publication of the 'Memoirs' I have held but little intercourse with the out-of-door world; perhaps less even than prior to that time. When I have gone from home it has been solely upon matters of business, and not with any view to either health or amusement. As this business usually called me to the same place, my road was generally the same, leading directly from my home to an avenue in the city of Westminster. It would be idle to narrate the particulars connected with more than a very few of these forced visits to the far-famed, but in my case not very inviting,

"Resort and mart of all the earth."

Should any of my readers know from experience the difficulty of transacting even a little business with inadequate means, they will not need to be told that these visits were commonly of an anxious, rather than of an entertaining character. As to journeying for the purpose of mere amusement, I have not done this for many a year. Indeed, I never leave home in quest of either bodily health or mental recreation. With respect to merely animal enjoyments, there are, as I believe, none that could improve my health; and it would be childish and censurable in me to make them, in any instance, the objects of my wishes or my earnest pursuit, as though I thought them to be necessary to my happiness; and in regard to mental pleasure, I am fully convinced that it would be nearly useless for one so full of bodily ailments and infirmities as myself, to look for much of it while engaged in the exercise of walking, especially in the crowded and noisy streets of a great city. In fact, I should wholly give up this kind of exercise, were I to be governed by my feelings rather than by a sense of duty. I could sometimes take a little rest in the National Gallery, and at the same time find employment for the imagination; but the difficulty of getting thither and an unwillingness to encounter the heated atmosphere of the rooms, are hindrances which are generally insurmountable.

Or, again, I might occasionally find recreation

in the reading-room at the British Museum, were it not that the little strength which I might have on setting out, would be so much exhausted by the journey—for to me it is truly a journey—that I should be unable to read with either pleasure or advantage. Further, my duties will not allow me to be long absent from home, and therefore I am the less inclined to avail myself of these resting-places, or even of those which now better serve my necessity, viz., the vestibule of the National Gallery and the lobby of the Museum reading-room. Thus it will readily appear that I neither look for nor find any great amount of amusement, or even of ease, during the time which I spend in London. In good truth I may affirm that I have lost the physical power which is needful for visiting places of public entertainment; although I have lost nothing of my predilection for the works of art or of learning. On the contrary, I should gladly avail myself of these sources of pure and delightful pleasure, were the body able to carry into effect either the purposes or the "desires of the mind."

There is yet another hindrance to my having out-of-door amusement; and this is the dislike I have to being in a crowd, as I am then unable to pursue my natural course of thought, or to give due play to the imagination. Moreover, I have no great confidence in the new modes of travelling on either land or water. I am afraid that they are not in general so safe as is desirable, especially to an invalid; and as I hold it to be morally wrong in one who has others to care for, to expose himself to danger, except in cases of necessity, I am very seldom a passenger in either a steam-ship or a railway carriage.

It will thus be seen that I have but few external sources of either instruction or amusement, and therefore it might seem, at first, as though I were in a very forlorn condition. This, however, I am not disposed to admit, for certainly I am not unhappy; on the contrary, I hesitate not to avow, I would not exchange the pleasure which is derivable from the seemingly unpromising sources that are within my reach for any amount of the childish, trifling, and irrational mirth which too frequently is dignified by the name of pleasure. I am bold to affirm that it is not only possible, but also comparatively easy, to draw much real enjoyment from the faithful performance of the every-day duties of social and domestic life. Thus much, indeed, is quite certain, that the review of any given portion of time spent in the discharge of these important and imperative duties will afford a vastly larger amount of mental satisfaction than can, under any circumstances, be drawn from the recollection of merely trifling and perhaps vitiating pleasures. To have contributed in any degree towards either the present or the future well-being of relatives or friends, or to have lent a helping hand to the great work of social improvement, whether physical or moral, must ever call up far more pleasurable reflections than any that can follow upon a course of mere amusement.

But there are other sources than these from which an invalid may derive much genuine and continuous satisfaction of heart, foremost among which is that which is afforded by a free and frequent correspondence with an intelligent and warm-hearted friend, especially if the friendship be of long standing. It is one of my chief privileges to enjoy the confidence and the genuine good-will of one whose friendship has endured through the long course of nearly forty years, and still continues as full and as cordial as ever. It is to this friend that allusion is made in a passage of the 'Memoirs' where, having noticed my fellow-workmen as but little worthy of esteem, an exception is made in favour of one concerning whom I felt called upon to report favourably.

It were superfluous to enlarge upon the value of friendship, as this is acknowledged by almost every one, although in too many instances its duties are little known and still less observed—the friend being scarcely more than a mere acquaintance. But when the important bearing of true friendship upon the happiness of man is considered, it is then seen how needful it is that just notions of its value and obligations should be entertained, by all who wish to number among their other sources of enjoyment that which consists in having a genuine friend.

"Poor is the friendless master of a world!"

is the exclamation of one who was well able to judge in this matter, and it would seem that his judgment was and yet is in agreement with facts, for it is reckoned as a great and almost peculiar drawback upon the happiness of the most exalted persons in society, that they have no friends. Whoever is at all conversant with the history of monarchs will readily admit that, except in a very few instances, friendship has not been an ingredient in their so-called "cup of felicity."

There are numerous rules to be found in the works of moralists in respect both to the choice of friends and the manner in which friends should treat each other, in order to the maintenance of such an amount of good-will, esteem, and confidence as may promote their mutual and individual happiness. As to the choice of friends, it would seem to be in general the result of experience, rather than of deliberate consideration. For example; two persons, before unknown to each other, are accidentally brought together, perhaps upon matters of business only, when each discovers in the other some qualities which give their possessor a good title to the esteem of his fellow-men. Thus they learn to regard one another with mutual feelings of good-will, which eventually ripen into a genuine and lasting friendship.

In passing I may venture to state, that I have not much faith in the genuineness of any of those professed friendships that are formed or maintained between persons of immoral character and habits. The whole current of the testimony given by frequently occurring facts goes to prove that the debasing principle of selfishness is the ruling law of such persons. Whenever, therefore, this principle is called into action, as it must often be in the case of criminal or deeply depraved people, there is an end at once to all their seeming friendship, and each one is ready to avow his belief that, notwithstanding all they have said to the contrary, self-preservation is the "first law of nature." I only add, that the ease with which such people consent to sacrifice those whom they have called "friends," when their own safety or other interests are in jeopardy, goes to confirm what has been said as to the impossibility of any real friendship existing between those in whom the feelings of genuine philanthropy have been destroyed by a course of demoralizing self-indulgence. Here, however, I must terminate these remarks, and advert to other subjects.

I have stated that I seldom go anywhere, except for purposes of business. This is strictly true;

yet there are instances in which I indulge myself with a slight view of some interesting exhibition. Thus it is, that sometimes, when I am near to the National Gallery, I go further than the vestibule, and employ myself for a short time in looking at the pictures; and as I contrive to do this while sitting, I compass two objects at the same time. I dare not presume to invade the province of the critic in regard to painting or sculpture, any more than in what relates to literature; yet I hope it may be allowable for even a plain uneducated man to give some description of such works of art as may come within his view, together with some account of their effect upon his imagination. So I shall take the liberty, when occasion offers, to tell the reader a little of my opinions on these matters.

Before I notice the works in the Gallery I will take a glance at the building itself, which has been much criticised, sometimes in a good-humoured, but more frequently in a very severe manner, as though it were devoid of all architectural merit, and totally unfit for the purposes to which it is applied. I must not venture to give an opinion upon a question that has been so much debated among the professors and patrons of architectural art; but I may be permitted to state that I think these censorious criticisms, even though they be free from bitterness, are much more unfriendly than the occasion seems to require. I also think they are faulty on other accounts. For instance, they appear to me to be given in too dictatorial a style, if the difficulty of deciding questions of taste and the fallibility of the critic be duly considered. Moreover, they seem to indicate an ungenerous, if not an unfair feeling towards the architect, who, after all, is probably little deserving of censure; while they appear to imply some degree of ingratitude towards a Government whose care in providing a place where the people might find gratuitous and rational entertainment entitles it to be cordially thanked, rather than even indirectly or slightly censured: for, if the edifice were unquestionably devoid of architectural beauty, or ill-adapted to answer the desired purposes, yet it would appear to deserve a charitable judgment, because of the very praiseworthy intentions of those who provided it. For myself, I venture to think that, in a case like this, were I able to judge accurately concerning architectural art, I should be disposed to aim at finding something which called for commendation rather than for censure; and I am slow to believe that the National Gallery has nothing about it which deserves to be commended.

These observations will, to a great extent, apply to the other arts. In regard to painting, it would be well were the critic to direct his chief attention to whatever may be praiseworthy in the picture before him, and when noticing its defects, to do so in a friendly spirit and in courteous language. This mode of criticism would answer the double purpose of encouraging and admonishing the artist, especially if he be a youthful one; while it would probably be far more instructive to the non-artistic admirer of pictures than either indiscriminate praise or unmeasured censure. These untaught admirers of pictures have, however, but little occasion to trouble themselves about matters of criticism. They go to an exhibition for the very natural and laudable purpose of finding amusement; and, in spite of whatever faults may be discoverable by the artist or the critic, they do not go on a bootless errand. So far as I am able to judge, I believe that all are gratified with what they see, although few could tell, or indeed stop to inquire, why they are so. It is not a little amusing to hear the comments which are frequently made. These comments, of course, have an almost exclusive reference to the subjects, rather than to the artistic merits of the pictures, and thus afford small occasion for any other than straightforward and familiar remarks, and these appear to be generally made in a spirit of genuine good-humour. For myself, I follow pretty nearly in the same track, as my object, like that of others, is entertainment; and therefore I look only for what may help me to obtain it. I may add, that I never look in vain, nor, indeed, have I to make a long search, for I am easily pleased; and where the means of pleasure are, as in this case, obtainable at little cost, I feel that it would be culpable to be otherwise. So long, therefore, as I do not see portraits which I know to be very unlike their originals, or historical pictures that greatly violate the truth of history, or landscapes which suggest the thought that they have not " their like" in nature, or imaginative pieces that imply contradictions or impossibilities, I am well enough pleased with what I see, and neither presume nor am disposed to meddle with " vexed questions" of taste or criticism.

I will now make a few remarks on some of the pictures in the Gallery; but here I shall be most careful to avoid assuming, or even seeming to assume, the character of a critic. My object is to assist such as myself so to observe the pictures as that they may derive from them all possible amusement and instruction. Beginning with the Scripture-pieces, I come first to the picture of 'Christ healing the Sick in the Temple.' Every one who is at all conversant with the history of Him " who went about doing good," may here find ample matter for thoughts of the deepest interest. The best feelings of the heart may here be brought into vigorous activity, —feelings of deep sympathy with human suffering—of earnest concern as to the moral diseases of which all physical maladies are at once the consequences and the symbols—and of fervent gratitude to Him who is justly called the " great and good physician." Besides all this, it were but natural that the picture should give rise to thoughts concerning the eminent man who painted it; such thoughts, moreover, as may lead to a wish for either learning or becoming more conversant with the history of his useful and honourable life. Thus it is that the spectator may derive both present and future entertainment from the contemplation of this or any similar work of art.

These remarks may easily be made applicable to the other Scriptural paintings in the Gallery, and therefore I need not stay to notice them. I will, however, suggest that the picture representing the Raising of Lazarus is adapted to awaken very important thoughts concerning a death far more dreadful than that of the body; and also concerning Him who is " the resurrection and the life," and who alone is able to raise man from a state of moral death to one of spiritual and immortal life.

As to the landscape pictures, they also may be made the sources of much genuine pleasure, apart from all consideration of their artistic merits. For example, they have power to carry the thoughts into the scenes of which, in their general features, they may be the exemplars; and thus, by pleasing the imagination with ideal prospects, make some compensation for the loss of rural pleasures to those who now can seldom ramble beyond " their brick-wall bounds." They have, moreover, another and a higher power, inasmuch as they tend to remind the spectator of Him who is the God of nature, and also the source of all its beauty and magnificence.

In like manner may the historical paintings be turned to the important purpose of instruction. The facts or events to which they refer are generally of sufficient interest to warrant the perusal of the histories from whence they were taken, and thus some desirable acquaintance with the history of either our own or a foreign country may be the result of what was intended by the spectator to be only an amusement. The same, or nearly so, may be said of the imaginative pieces, as these also may be made to produce a wish for some knowledge of the fabulous subjects to which they relate; and in this way amusement may again become the handmaid of useful knowledge.*

In regard to the pictures which represent national customs or domestic economy, I need not say much in order to show their useful tendency, while

* I venture to call this knowledge "useful," because of the representative character of mythological history. If this be kept in mind, it will readily be seen that these fables may involve much of genuine and important truth.

nothing requires to be said as to their amusing character. I will therefore confine myself to the expression of an earnest wish that Hogarth's two pictures, called respectively 'Gin Lane' and 'Beer Street,' could be added to those of that eminently instructive artist which are already in the Gallery. My reasons for this wish are too obvious to call for any explanatory remark. Of the portraits in this collection I shall say nothing further than that I hope they so accurately resemble their originals, as to give a clue towards the discovery of something connected either with their intellectual or their moral character.

Here I quit the National Gallery, in and about which I have stayed too long to allow of my taking more than a hasty glance at several adjacent works of art. The chief of these are the Nelson Monument, the equestrian statues of Charles I. and George IV., and the Fountains. I say nothing of the latter, except that I am very well pleased with them. As to the statues, I will presently make a brief reference to that of George IV.; but as to the Nelson Column, I have an objection which I will venture to note at greater length—premising, however, that my faith in its validity is not very strong. Judging as a non-artistic man, I am doubtful as to the propriety of placing a statue upon the top of a single and lofty column, or, indeed, upon that of any other architectural work of great altitude; because the spectator is thereby prevented from contemplating the figure, which, however, should be the proper or the chief object of attraction. Moreover, it implies a great degree of improbability (if not, indeed, what is plainly impossible), and thus tends to disturb the equable or tranquil feelings with which works of art ought to be contemplated. In this case I am sometimes a little disturbed, for, in spite of all my efforts to the contrary, I am led to ask myself how it was that the statue—which for the moment I seem to regard as having life—could have performed a climbing exploit which so far exceeds the ordinary strength or skill of a human being.

As I am now in the neighbourhood, it might seem well to notice the column and statue raised in honour of the late Duke of York; but, as what has been said of the Nelson Monument is equally applicable to this, I pass on to look at the Wellington Equestrian Statue, about which there has been so much of eager, if not angry, controversy. Here, also, my objections to the column come upon me, and I am tempted to inquire whether it was ever known that a man on horseback contrived to get upon the roof of a rather lofty building, having perpendicular walls, and, if so, for what purpose it was that he performed this singular and arduous feat. I am fearful of violating my purpose of not assuming to be a critical judge on questions of taste, or I might here venture to suggest that a far more suitable pedestal for this statue than its present one might, perhaps, have been found on or near the summit of a large and rugged mass of rock, similar to that upon which stands the equestrian statue of Peter the Great in the Russian metropolis. In thus placing it, there could have been no idea of an impossibility, if, indeed, of any great improbability, suggested by its position; while that position would be suggestive of far greater difficulties than this having been surmounted by a resolute and persevering spirit.

Craving the reader's forbearance, I will make one more remark before I finally dismiss these subjects. This relates to equestrian statues, wherein both man and horse are represented in a state of total inaction. To me they seem, when thus represented, to be devoid of all interesting expressiveness or meaning; while they much resemble what, in real life, has a very undignified appearance. Thus, the statue in memory of George IV., in Trafalgar-square, together with that in Cornhill, in honour of the Duke of Wellington, compels me to think of a groom about to give exercise to his master's horse, rather than of a powerful monarch or a celebrated warrior. If, however, it be thought desirable that these works should sometimes be thus executed, it is, I think, possible to avoid that unimpressive aspect to which I have referred. There is an incident recorded in the 'Memoirs' of that worthily-celebrated man—the late Mr. Samuel Drew—which, I venture to suggest, might supply the sculptor with a very apt subject for the representation of an inactive state, unaccompanied by any tameness of expression. As I quote from memory, I shall probably fail to give the precise words of the author; but I hope that what follows will embody the substance of the story. It appears that Mr. Drew's sister, having occasion to visit a place at a considerable distance from her home, went thither on horseback. On her return, she attempted to shorten her journey by going over the sea-beach, the tide being then at ebb. Before, however, she could effect her purpose, it began to flow. In a short time she was unable to make any further progress, as the remaining space was too much for her horse to traverse by swimming. In this extremity, she endeavoured to get beyond the high-water mark; but here another difficulty presented itself—the shore was precipitous and rocky, so that there was no landing-place. Meanwhile the tide continued to rise, placing both horse and rider in great jeopardy. The horse made an energetic effort to save himself, by climbing the rocks, and so far succeeded as to escape being drowned, although his hinder parts were immersed in the water. He retained his hold until the tide had receded sufficiently to allow of his descending from his nove and perilous elevation—a task of considerable difficulty and danger, but which was at length safely performed. During the whole of this fearful adventure his rider kept close to him, for the double purpose of giving him encouragement and securing herself. Now, in such an example as this, the sculptor might, as I presume to think, find ample scope for representing a state of inaction, relieved of all tameness, by its conveying a powerful idea of previous and violent exertion.

Here, however, I close these seeming criticisms, and, in doing so, earnestly request that whatever I may have said which may appear to be critical, may nevertheless be regarded as no more than the opinion of a plain and untaught man.

CHAPTER IV.

I HAVE already intimated my gratitude to the Government for having given to the people the means of obtaining amusement; yet I must allow myself the pleasure of again expressing it on account of some other instances in which its benevolent care has been evinced. I shall first name that of the pleasure-grounds in St. James's Park, which some years ago were made free for public use, after having been laid out in a manner which, to any one who remembers them in their previous state, can hardly fail of seeming beautiful. It is now truly gratifying to look at these grounds when they have in them their usual number of visitors, many of whom could not get either pleasant or healthful exercise but for the facilities afforded by these inviting and convenient gardens. Another instance is that of the Green Park, which also has been made a pleasant and an easily accessible place of public resort. To these I will add another, viz. that of the improvements made in Hyde Park for the same praiseworthy purpose.

It is so pleasant to find cause for commendation in those who in general have but little praise given to them (while they meet with abundance of censure), that I must advert to yet another instance in which our rulers have shown their good-will to the people. This relates to the "School of Design" at Somerset House—to which, although it is not what is commonly called "a public exhibition," there is, nevertheless, free admission for the public at fixed hours. Whoever visits it, with a view to rational amusement, will not be disappointed. Being one day in its neighbourhood at the proper time, I looked in, and had no reason to regret having done so. There were but few students then present, it being, as I suppose, their meal-time; this, however, was perhaps an advantage rather than otherwise, for I was thereby able to take a more complete view of what was going on, as also of the accommodations provided for the students, some of whom were employed in drawing and others in modelling. My conclusion from what I saw is, that any one who wishes for instruction in the "arts of design," but who is not able to become a student, may turn even an occasional visit to a useful purpose.

Having thus briefly alluded to what the Government has done towards providing rational amusement for the people, I turn to what has been supplied with a similar view by private liberality. I will not, however, multiply examples, but confine myself to one only, which I select because I believe

E

it to be worthy of especial notice by all working men who have a desire to obtain rational entertainment when they are free from the calls of their necessary occupation. Many of these are glad to escape—although it be but for a brief season—not only from the unhealthy workshop or factory, but also from the "close-pent" courts or the dark alleys in which they are forced to have their habitations. Such will do well, when they go abroad,

"To range the fields and treat their lungs with air,"

to visit the delightful hamlet of Dulwich. When they get fairly out of the metropolis they will find their pathway a right pleasant one, whether they take the public road or go across the fields. In addition to its many other attractions, there is in this hamlet a large collection of beautiful paintings, which may be seen, free of expense, on any day except Friday and Sunday. If wearied by the walk, they may rest (while looking at the pictures) upon commodious seats. I doubt not that they will be much pleased with this excursion, especially should they be exempt from the almost overpowering influence of bodily infirmity by which I was oppressed while on my homeward journey. It may not be superfluous to note that the admission to the exhibition is by tickets, which, however, are easily obtainable on application to many of the chief printsellers of London. Those who are not family-men would not do amiss to visit Dulwich on the Sunday, provided they attend public worship; and for this attendance—so highly important in itself, and so truly delightful to every right-minded person—there is ample convenience in the chapel of the college to which the picture-gallery belongs. This college is a very noble charitable institution, founded in the year 1614, by one who is said to have been an eminent dramatic performer. He afterwards became the proprietor of several places of public amusement, by which he gained so much money as enabled him to build and liberally endow this college, to which, with equal piety and modesty, he gave the finely expressive name of "God's Gift."

By a natural connexion of thought I am here reminded of another charitable institution—of equally admirable character—the Charterhouse, to which, although it be not a public exhibition, I once gained access, and which, from that time, I have been free to visit, though as yet I have not been able to avail myself of this privilege. The way in which I was led thither was as follows:—About forty years ago I read a duodecimo volume, in which was given an account of the author's travels in the United States of America. The book, though small, contained, as I thought, a large amount of valuable and highly amusing information. I could not retain the copy which I read, as it was hired; but I felt so strong a desire to possess myself of the work, as to be put upon making a long-continued search for that purpose. All was, however, of no avail, as I could not at that time meet with a second copy. A few years ago I made another search, but with the like ill-success. Among many other places, I visited the shop at which I had hired the copy referred to. It was kept by the same persons, and the stock of books appeared to be the same, as in 1810. The good people told me that they believed such a book was somewhere in the shop, but where to look for it they could not tell. I could very easily believe this, as the general appearance of what had once been a *moving* library, but which evidently had long been a *resting* one, plainly showed that the work of discovering and disinterring the book in question was far too difficult for the aged and infirm people to whom it belonged: so I gave over my search, although my desire to gain what I had been looking after remained with me in all its force. One incident or another would constantly bring this book before the " inward eye," and thus contribute to keep alive my wish to obtain it. At length I learned from the newspapers that Her Majesty the Queen had given a Charterhouse presentation to a gentleman who was stated to have been a great traveller in various countries, among which was named North

America. He was further stated to have been the author of some valuable books. The name of this gentleman corresponding with that of the author of my much-coveted volume, coupled with the announcement that he had travelled in America, led me to resolve upon trying to see him. I had not, however, any very sanguine hopes of getting a copy of his book by this means—being of opinion that authors rarely peruse their own works after publication, and yet more rarely preserve copies of them for nearly half a century. Yet I considered that I might perhaps get some refreshment for the memory, and moreover some additional information, could I but gain access to the author. So I went to the Charterhouse, where I was soon shown the way to his room, and met with a very frank and courteous reception, which encouraged me to be somewhat free in my inquiries. In passing, I may remark that the opinions adopted by this gentleman concerning the government, the institutions, and the people of the United States, seem to me to have been fully borne out, both by subsequent events and the present state of the American Republic.

After having looked over the large, lofty, and in all respects comfortable room occupied by my host, and partaken of the food provided for him, he took me into the chapel, the dining-hall, and other parts of the institution, where I saw what filled me with " great admiration " of the founder's piety towards God and large-heartedness towards his fellow-men. Whoever wishes for a full and also a very interesting account of this princely charity, may find it in a number of that justly esteemed publication, 'Chambers' Edinburgh Journal;' I cannot give the date, but I think it must have been published somewhere about three or four years ago. To that account I refer the reader, as it is very far superior in all respects to any that I could give. I must not, however, omit to notice the fact, that this institution, as in the case of Dulwich College, has never borne the name of its founder, having been originally called " King James's College," in honour of the monarch in whose reign it was founded.

In regard to the worthy individual to whose kindness I was indebted for the view of what I found to be so highly interesting, I have only to add, that although an aged man, he was, when I saw him, both healthy and active. He told me that he was a stranger to sickness and disease, notwithstanding that he had travelled much in regions which are considered to be unfavourable to health, and had endured much of the hardship to which travellers are usually exposed. This freedom from bodily ailments he attributed, in a great degree, to his custom of water-drinking, which he had practised for more than forty years.

It may, perhaps, have been remarked that I make

no mention of any other than gratuitous exhibitions; my reason for this is twofold; first, because I doubt the prudence of working men spending any part of their income in " sight-seeing," especially when, as is now the case, there is so much which is really interesting to be seen without charge; and secondly, because I have no great confidence in the announcements concerning many public shows, which, if unquestionably genuine, might perhaps be worth looking at. As to those which rank with the Hottentot Venus and the Siamese Twins of former days, together with the Tom Thumb of more recent date, I consider them to be altogether disgusting, when considered as general exhibitions, and, moreover, cannot but think that they tend to foster a morbid taste for what is merely wonderful, if not, indeed, repulsively monstrous, and thus prove to be great obstacles in the way of forming or confirming a love for what is truly entertaining, and, at the same time, rationally instructive.

This leads me to remark, that, although I have referred to the public exhibitions of paintings, and other works of art, as providing for the rational amusement of the people, I do not feel satisfied that mere amusement ought to be the end of any human pursuit. Life is a warfare, in which every intelligent being is called upon to be, more or less, a combatant; and,

" Who wants amusement in the flame of battle ?"

It ought, therefore, to be the main object of every one of sound mind, to be continually on the lookout for what may be useful in carrying on this warfare, from which, as there is no exemption, so neither is there any way of escape, unless recourse be had to a hermit-life in some vast and solitary wilderness.

If, indeed, this needful knowledge can be gained through an entertaining or inviting medium, there is no objection to be made against such a mode of obtaining it; but, if this be not practicable, it then becomes imperatively binding upon a moral agent, who, be it remembered, is also an accountable being, to learn the art of making what is a duty a source of real pleasure. This art is not so difficult of acquirement as many would suppose; of which there is abundant proof in the cases of not a few of our species, who have given to the world full evidence that they never lacked amusement, although their time was almost unceasingly employed in earnest application to some business or study that called for the habitual exercise of patient, if not, indeed, of laborious thought. These truly honourable persons were happy, in the best sense of that often misused word, for they were conscious of being engaged in pursuits which tended to promote the general and permanent well-being of others: and whoever feels this consciousness, cannot fail of being far more than merely entertained. On the contrary, those who pursue amusement only, are in great danger of not only failing to obtain it, but also of involving themselves, and perhaps others also (who may be dependent upon them) in much of real perplexity and discomfort.

Of this I knew a notable example, in the case of a fellow-workman, whom I will venture to call

THE AMUSEMENT HUNTER.

He was, in many respects, a praiseworthy man, being of temperate habits, a good workman, fairly intelligent upon many subjects, of a good temper and becoming manners. He was, moreover, a family-man, and seemed to be truly attached to his wife and children. But there was a serious drawback upon all his good qualities in his inordinate love of amusement. By this he was often drawn, first, into self-deception, and then, as the necessary consequence of such deception, into a wrong course of action. He had, it appeared, been formerly connected with a company of strolling players, whose manner of life, albeit of a thriftless and vagrant character, seems to have very considerable attractions for many. This was the case with my workfellow, who, in spite of past experience, and at the hazard of incurring both trouble and loss, often persuaded himself that he could " turn a penny," by giving theatrical entertainments, of which he himself was so ardent a lover. These speculations usually turned out very unfortunately for his pocket, involving him in debt which he was ill able to discharge, and hindering him from following his proper business, at which he might have earned good wages. He then had to endure the pangs of useless regret, which, judging from the symptoms that he usually manifested, seem to have been acute. To these self-reproaches were often added the severe rebukes of his more prudent shopmates or the provoking taunts of those among them who loved to inflict pain. At length he grew tired of his theatrical pursuits, and then took to verse-making. On one occasion he wrote a piece, which he called 'The Theatre,' with copious notes, for the purpose of illustrating or confirming the facts recorded in the text. I do not venture to say more of the versification, than that it was, as I judged, quite equal to much that finds its way into print; but as to the sentiments, they were really deserving of approbation. The piece was prefaced by a dedication, in a rather theatrical style, addressed to a most worthy gentleman, a minister of the Established Church. But he went no further than this, in his literary course, as he had not the means of getting his poem through the press.

He had now to discover some new source of entertainment. As he had a talent for mimicry, he found a good deal of amusement in imitating the gait or the general manners of his workfellows, to the no small annoyance of some; while others were made merry by seeing themselves, as it were, in a mirror, which, while it gave a somewhat distorted reflection, yet preserved a general resemblance to the original. At other times, he employed himself in collecting all the gossiping information that he could obtain; and this he would often use to a rather troublesome extent. Then he affected Odd-Fellowship, all the so-called secrets of which he would, with great glee, divulge to his brethren of the shopboard. This, however, often led to angry feeling on the part of other members of the Odd Fellows' club, but he enjoyed their manifestations of wrath, and could, at all times, easily conquer them in a battle of mere words.

All these resources, however, failed to satisfy the cravings of his wayward fancy, and, therefore, were successively discarded, while he set out in quest of some new object wherewith to supply their place. In this last adventure he happily met with one which could not be easily exhausted, while it had the merit of being truly instructive as well as entertaining.

My worthy friend before mentioned was a collector of curious insects, and often, in examining specimens, which to him were new, used a small microscope. The accounts which he gave of his discoveries by this means attracted the attention of my hero, who, forthwith, set himself to the work of insect collecting. By the aid of my friend's instrument, which was freely lent to him, he greatly added to the pleasure given him by his new pursuit. He often made short excursions into the adjacent country, and seldom returned without bringing with him some entomological specimens which were new to himself, and, sometimes, to my friend also. Ere long, he was master of a collection of insects; with which, together with numerous pieces of green turf, wild-flower plants, and other productions of the fields, he ornamented the little room in which he lived, so as to make it one of the prettiest, as it also was one of the cleanest and neatest, apartments that I have ever seen. All this was well, if not, indeed, highly praiseworthy; and, could he have continued to regard the study of insects as being, in his case, fitting only for an amusement, there could have been no harm done; while, perhaps, some real good might have been produced. But in this, as in other instances, he was led to aim at making his living dependent upon what was wholly inadequate for that purpose.

Before he had fully entered upon his new speculation, we were separated, I think, by my removing to London; and thus I lost sight of him for several years. At length I re-encountered him in the following rather curious manner. In the hot summer of 1818, while indulging myself with an afternoon's recreation, I was in the act of crossing Hyde Park, on my way to Kensington Gardens, which I had nearly reached, when I observed a large instrument, which turned out to be a solar microscope, standing upon the greensward, without, as it seemed, having any one to watch over its safety. Soon, however, I discovered a man stretched at full length upon the grass with his face uppermost. This proved to be my former workfellow, who was now engaged in the calling of an insect exhibitor. He instantly recognised me, and, giving me a most hearty welcome, insisted upon my seeing some of the wonderful objects of which he was the possessor. I am bound to say the " sight " was well worth seeing. His instrument, being of a highly magnifying power, enabled him to show me many specimens of animalcula, some of which were truly surprising, while the whole, viewed collectively, was well adapted to produce a feeling of devout admiration in regard to the wisdom of their great Creator. We then parted, and I heard no more of him until after a considerable lapse of time; when, as I was proceeding along the Edgware Road, I observed a small cottage having a large showboard affixed to its front, upon which were written in very conspicuous characters the words " Grand Solar Exhibition." Beneath this, in smaller letters, appeared an extract from the 'Morning Hymn' of Milton's Adam:—

"These are thy glorious works, parent of good!"

and so on. By these significant tokens I was reminded of my old acquaintance, and concluded that he was the proprietor or manager of this magnificent display. I could not then call, in order to verify my conjecture, but afterwards found that it was a correct one. I once more lost all trace of him, until, on a dreary winter evening, I again met with him as I was going home after the conclusion of my day's work. He had then resumed his proper business, since all his efforts to procure a maintenance by his exhibition had turned out to be worse than useless. As usual, he was very poorly clad; but he was, as he had ever been, clean in his person, and decent in his general appearance. He was in deep grief at the time, on account of the death of one of his children, and told me, with much emotion, that he considered this bereavement in the light of a Divine judgment upon him, because of his many sins.

From that time until now, a period of more than thirty years, I have neither seen nor heard of him; nevertheless, I think it probable that he is yet in this life; and if so, I should be much pleased at meeting with him. Should he chance to see the outline of his character which I have here sketched,

I doubt not that he will recognise some traces of the hand that drew it. He will, I am sure, fully acquit me of all ill-feeling towards him, and acknowledge that, while I have not flattered him, by attributing to him qualities which he did not possess, so neither have I caricatured him by giving a distorted or grotesque portrait. Most glad should I be to learn that now, when like myself he is becoming an old man, he has settled down into staid and sober-minded habits. Meanwhile I venture to hold him up as an admonitory example of the evils consequent upon an inordinate love of mere amusement.

CHAPTER V.

After what I have advanced in favour of popular knowledge, it may not be out of place if I here advert to the now much-mooted question of popular ignorance, a question vastly momentous, inasmuch as it involves the safety and the happiness of the whole community. Ignorance, crime, and misery necessarily go together, and it is an incontrovertible fact that the most profound ignorance upon every subject connected with man's best interests prevails among many myriads of even a London population, notwithstanding its general pretensions to superior intelligence. Of the adult portion of these myriads there is, I fear, but little warrant for believing that it will ever become much better instructed than it now is. Life is too short, and human power too limited, for the accomplishment of a task at once so arduous and so vast as that of duly instructing such a multitude of thoroughly ignorant people. As to the youthful portion, however, there is better cause for hoping that it may, if properly cared for, become fairly instructed, both in morals and secular knowledge, especially if some way should be discovered whereby it might escape from the baneful influence of demoralizing and debasing example. It is one of the most cheering signs of the times, that a large number of able and rightly-disposed persons have, at length, become aware of the worse than merely brutish ignorance and sensuality that so widely prevail, and are doing all that in them lies towards enlightening and morally elevating their wretchedly degraded fellow-beings.

But the work is almost astoundingly laborious and difficult, because of its vast magnitude, and also of the many formidable obstacles that oppose its progress. Yet there is no cause for despair. What has already been effected is sufficient to inspire a confidence of yet greater success. If the work be carried on by those who will remember that it demands all the labour that can be brought to bear upon it, they will not waste either their time or their powers in finding fault with each other, or in crossing each other's path. All will, probably, sometimes fall into a wrong course; all, therefore, must be forbearing and charitably disposed, so that they may work in unison, " with one heart," if not with one mind, or no real good can be produced by their otherwise praiseworthy exertions. There will, perhaps, be proposed many schemes for bettering the people's condition; some of which will, evidently, be mere nostrums, while others may, if brought into action, turn out to be greatly inadequate for the required purpose, though not without their use, in preparing the way for better contrived and more effective measures. Above all things, it should be well understood and remembered that there can be no permanent amelioration of the people's domestic or social condition until their moral constitution is so far renovated as to allow their mental energies to be brought into a state of healthy and well-directed action. The work of genuine reformation must begin with individuals, and, in every case, it must begin at the heart, or there can be no permanent good effected. All that may be done in the way of either political reform or social improvement will be of no real utility, unless the public mind be previously well instructed in the principles of genuine truth and goodness. The work of communicating, or rather, of disseminating these principles, where the soil has hitherto remained unbroken, will assuredly prove both laborious and difficult. The accumulated ignorance of many centuries is not to be removed in a day, nor by any but the most strenuous and persevering efforts. To such as are duly qualified for this great work, I need say nothing as to the ineffectiveness of all human efforts, unless they be directed and aided by Him who is at once " wonderful in counsel and excellent in working." But I forbear to enlarge; observing, however, that *thus* far my remarks have been confined to that large class of persons which, although thoroughly ignorant and fearfully depraved, nevertheless forms the foundation upon which rests the whole social edifice. How perilous must be the condition of that edifice while its basis is thus unsound, and, moreover, pregnant with combustible matter, I will not attempt to show; I will, however, venture to recommend the subject to the most serious consideration of the Christian philanthropist, whatever may be his rank in society.

'Instances of the ignorance and viciousness which abound in the class to which I refer, have often come under my notice. In some cases, I have endeavoured to ascertain something of the individual's intellectual and moral state; and the result has been such as to convince me that we have among us a multitude of beings whose chief claim to be regarded as human seems to consist in their external form, so completely are the understanding blinded and the will corrupted. The difficulty of dealing with these formidable evils is much increased by the fact, that they are not confined to the lowest class of the people. They prevail to no trifling extent among the classes that occupy a superior rank. Thus, among mechanics, and other handicraftsmen, vast numbers are almost totally ignorant upon the supremely important subjects of morals and religion. It is not going beyond the truth to affirm that by far the greater number of these people never enter the places where they might obtain instruction upon these and other branches of necessary and truly desirable knowledge. It is lamentable to see how they waste their leisure time, especially their Sundays; which to a working man are in so many respects of incalculable value. Attired in their dirty, and often ragged, working garments, they loiter about the public ways, or congregate, when arrives the much longed-for hour of opening them, in the houses where " strong drink" may be obtained. Here they spend no inconsiderable amount of their earnings in gratifying their sensual and morally debasing appetites, to the utter neglect of all the best interests of both themselves and their families.

If the subject of religion be made the topic of conversation, as it often is in tippling companies, it is in general only that it may be laughed at, or treated with the most bitter and hearty contempt. Happily there are many exceptions to this too general rule, and these exceptions are increasing; but even here there is much cause for regret, because, although the minds of many are being instructed in useful science, the noblest and the most valuable of all sciences, that of religion, is either totally neglected or despised and discarded. Yet it were not difficult to show, that whatever branch of knowledge is either hostile to this paramount science or in no way sanctioned by it is, to the full extent of this hostility or want of sanction, defective in its power of compassing the only proper end of all true knowledge, that of training the human mind for genuine usefulness in this life, and, indirectly at least, for the felicitous avocations of that which is to come.

But I must not enlarge upon this topic further than to observe, first, that if I seem to have been severe, I have not gone beyond the truth; and, secondly, that if I be thought to have derived my conclusions from insufficient premises, my answer must be, that I once belonged to a trade club, held at what was popularly known as a "house of call," which sometimes numbered from seven to eight hundred members. I am bold to say that, with the exception of perhaps fifty, who were Roman Catholics, and who in general attended the morning service of their church, not twenty paid any regard whatever to religious worship, nor in any other way recognised the claims of religion. I have been guided by this fact, in coming to a conclusion upon the general question, and I think that I am fully warranted in so doing, as men of other trades are not known to be more attentive to the great subjects of morals and religion than are those of my own. I will only add, that I have no reason to believe that they are now in a more hopeful state than they were at the time alluded to.

I now come to another class of persons, among whom there are numerous instances of profound ignorance upon every subject except that of their own calling; and even in this they are often so ill instructed, in respect of the principles upon which it ought to be conducted, as to make it the instrument of deteriorating, rather than of improving, both their intellectual powers and their moral feelings. All this may seem to be harsh, but it is too true to be successfully controverted. I will give one or two examples of the very disreputable, because voluntary ignorance, which may even now be found in men belonging to this class.

About five or six years ago, while conversing with a tradesman, who then was carrying on a good business, our discourse happened to turn upon books, when he affirmed, and seemingly with perfect sincerity, that he could not perceive or imagine the utility of any book whatever, unless it were a day-book or a ledger; from which observation the reader will readily estimate the amount of either secular or religious knowledge which he possessed.

Another example is that of a tradesman, a family man, by whom I was gravely told a similar tale, as to his not being able to see any utility in books; and who added that, even with respect to children, not excepting his own, he could not believe that they were at all needful or desirable. Being a little startled at this avowal, I doubted whether he spoke seriously, and therefore questioned him somewhat closely upon the subject. The manner in which he answered these questions convinced me that he was quite in earnest. Meanwhile (and I beg the reader's especial attention to this particular) he expressed a deliberate and full belief that it was really good for himself to eat heartily of animal food at supper-time, and moreover to drink freely afterwards of ardent spirits; yet at this very time he was in no small danger of being attacked by that formidable disorder which in a multitude of instances

"cramm'd intemperance knocks
Down to the ground at once, as butcher felleth ox."

I ventured to advise him as to the pressing necessity, in his case, of strict temperance, both in eating and drinking, when he made that common yet truly humiliating confession, that he could not deny himself these gratifications; and thus our conference ended.

To these examples I could, were it needful, add many others, but I forbear; merely observing, that I have met with men of the same class, who were almost totally ignorant upon the most familiar subjects; such, for instance, as the principal events, or the most celebrated persons, recorded in either sacred or secular history, not excepting even that of their own country. But this is an unpleasing subject; and I hasten to quit it for one of a more inviting aspect. Ere, however, I finally dismiss it, I must say a little in the way of excuse for the ignorance upon which I have been remarking, which, in many instances, it is but fair to suppose, has not been altogether voluntary. It is not very long ago that the means of easily acquiring useful knowledge were, for the first time, placed fairly within the reach of the poorer classes of society, to which many, who now hold the rank of master-tradesmen, originally belonged. Thus, at the only proper time for beginning to acquire knowledge, they were, to a great extent, destitute of the means; meanwhile, not a few of those who, from their rank and education, ought to have recognised its high value, and to have promoted its dissemination among the people, were either quite careless of their duty, or directly hostile to popular instruction. In my own case, I well remember to have been repeatedly scolded for having given some signs of wishing for book-knowledge. These rebukes, being given by an aged man, were on that account very unseemly; but they were made much more so, by reason of the rebuker having for many years been a bookseller, and who was then living at his ease upon the profits of his former trade. Under these adverse and often positively discouraging circumstances, it is perhaps not surprising that so many men of mature age, and now of respectable condition, should be so greatly deficient as they are in regard to knowledge. Except in the comparatively few instances where there there was, on the part of a poor boy, a strong natural desire for intellectual instruction, it was little likely that any voluntary efforts would be made in order to acquire it; while it was still less so that any sacrifices would be submitted to for that purpose. After an individual has passed through the seasons of childhood and early youth, without having been duly instructed, it is rarely that any considerable, or even merely adequate, amount of knowledge is obtained. In many instances, there is no convenient means of getting it; while, in yet more numerous cases, there is no desire for it, because there is no power of perceiving its value, either as a source of rational entertainment, or as the means of adding weight to the influence of character or condition.

Here I take leave of this topic, upon which I have, perhaps, dwelt too long; yet if my remarks should be the means of subserving the true interests of any who are now growing up in ignorance, and who, consequently, are in danger of becoming either positively vicious or grossly sensual, I may, as I hope, stand excused for my prolixity.

CHAPTER VI.

I now resume my narrative, which, as the reader may perhaps remember, has not yet been brought beyond the middle of the year 1845. In the spring of that year I lost a kind patron, by the decease of the late Mr. Thomas Hood, the justly-celebrated author. To this gentleman I had been known for several years, during which time I had his full permission to wait upon him whenever I wished to do so. It was however but seldom that I could avail myself of this privilege, for a privilege it certainly was. When I could thus indulge myself, I invariably met with a most courteous and encouraging reception, both from himself and Mrs. Hood, and I shall not, I hope, ever cease gratefully to remember my honoured and kind friends. Mr. Hood's conversation was to me highly interesting, and it was my own fault if it were not also very instructive. There was nothing about it of that light and jocular kind which many might have supposed; on the contrary, it was as grave and earnest as it well could be, and, moreover, marked by indications of such feelings as were, in my view, highly honourable to him. I fully believe him to have been a genuine philanthropist; ready at all times, and in all practicable ways, to aim at increasing the comforts and promoting the true interests of humanity. Of his deeply earnest sympathy with human suffering, his 'Song of the Shirt' affords an affecting and convincing proof. This sympathy was the more honourable to him, as he was, when he wrote that song, heavily burdened by cares, and borne down by severe bodily disease. He was, indeed, at all times very much afflicted by physical pain and disorder; so that I could not but wonder at his making such arduous literary exertions as those in which he was almost incessantly engaged. I can truly affirm that I never saw such another instance of the power of mind over matter as I witnessed in the case of this gentleman. After his decease I was favoured with the continued good will of his widow, who employed me to make clothes for her son, and, in other ways, gave me full proof of her wish to promote my well being. I take great pleasure in recording the grateful sense which I retain of all the kindnesses shown to me by her and Mr. Hood. I have some books which they gave me, among which is a copy of that valuable work, 'The Rambler,' by Dr. Johnson; and I hardly need to add that I carefully preserve these memorials of their kindly feelings.

I am here led to remark, that it was through

Mr. Hood's courtesy that I had an opportunity of becoming acquainted with the history and the writings of Mr. Charles Lamb, a gentleman whom I judge to have been a very worthy person, as well as a justly-eminent author. The perusal of his works, and also of his memoirs, gave me much pleasure. By the same courtesy I was permitted to read some of the works of Mr. Lamb's amiable and gifted sister, who, under the feigned name of Mrs. Leicester, contributed many pieces of mingled entertainment and instruction, for the use and benefit of young people. I was also allowed to peruse one of Mr. Lamb's manuscript letters. It was a very amusing epistle; and the more so, because of its containing two figures, which the writer affirms are the nearest approaches he could make towards the delineation of the human form. They were meant to represent himself and his sister. I forbear to give copies, as it will suffice to observe that they were respectively made up of a circle and five straight lines, from which description the reader's imagination will easily form an image, not very unlike the original drawings.

I am here reminded of having been permitted, by another honoured patron, to read a very long letter written by that able and good man the late Mr. Samuel Drew. It was chiefly filled with curious information relative to the traditions and customs of the people of Cornwall, Mr. Drew's native county. There was also an account of the architectural and other antiquities then existing in the vicinity of the writer's native place. I have, in my former book, stated that I had read the 'Memoirs' of this justly-distinguished man; and I here take an opportunity of recommending them to the attentive perusal of all who wish to acquire knowledge, but who want the proper leisure, and other requisites, for obtaining it. In Mr. Drew's personal history they will not fail of seeing how effectually a resolute and patient mind can overcome all obstacles that are not necessarily insurmountable. The prudence of this eminent man was evinced by his avoiding the rock upon which so many self-instructed authors have split. He did not suffer his literary tastes to interfere with his proper duties, but continued, long after he became an author, to look for a maintenance from his worldly calling, regarding literature rather as an amusement than as a source of pecuniary profit. Subsequently he was engaged wholly in literary pursuits, but even then his practical wisdom was evident; for he did not employ himself at his own risk, or on mere speculation, but was retained at a competent salary as the editor of a respectable periodical publication. By acting in this considerate manner he secured himself against that humiliating poverty and heart-consuming vexation which have been endured by many whose sad history is too well known to require that I should record their names.

It may readily be seen that authors of this class should regard literature as a crutch to be used occasionally, rather than as a staff whereon to trust entirely for support. There are some remarks upon this subject by those eminent authors Lord Byron and Mr. Charles Lamb, which strike me as being singularly just and forcible. His lordship, on being asked for his advice as to the querist's giving up a permanent and sufficiently remunerating situation, so that he might apply himself wholly to literary pursuits, thus answers him:—

"You know what ills the author's life assail—
Toil, envy, want, the patron, and the jail."

"Do not renounce writing, but never trust entirely to authorship. If you have a profession, retain it, and it will be, like Prior's fellowship, a last and sure resource." Mr. Lamb, in answer to the same person, says, "If you have but five consolatory minutes between the desk and the bed, make much of them, and live a century in them, rather than turn slave to the booksellers. I have known many authors want for bread, some repining, others enjoying the blessed security of a sponging-house; all agreeing they had rather have been tailors, weavers—what not?—rather than the things they were. I have known some starved, some go mad; one dear friend literally dying in a workhouse! You know not—may you never know—the miseries of subsisting by authorship!" (See 'Lamb's Letters,' vol. ii. page 88.) This excellent advice was followed, and thus the worthy and gifted man referred to was happily preserved from becoming liable to the evils which Mr. Lamb so forcibly depicts. He has continued, and, I believe, still continues, to earn his living at the desk; but he has not lost his taste for literature, as is sufficiently testified by the several works which since then he has sent into the world.

For myself, I have no great reason to complain of either the "pains" or the "perils" of authorship; but it must be remembered, first, that I never abandoned nor neglected my proper business for the sake of being a professional author; and, secondly, that I providentially fell into the hands of a gentleman who, as I fully believe, had no wish to serve himself without at the same time serving me. If all publishers were of a like spirit, there would be much less of the poverty and unhappiness now so common among the poorer classes of authors. Yet, notwithstanding all the benefit which has been permitted to follow my humble literary efforts, I would, were I able to do "a day's work in a day," much rather make or mend clothes than attempt to make books, provided, however, that I could get, as I once could, a "fair day's wages for a fair day's work." In this case I should be enabled to follow my little book-making business without anxiety as to the pecuniary issue; and thus it would be simply an amusement, whereas it has hitherto been an imperative duty, as I was unable to earn money by any other means. Yet, although it was toilsome, it was not repulsive, for it gave promise of being useful. This promise was in each instance fulfilled, and to a much greater extent than I could have ventured to look for. As to the "pains and penalties" of authorship in the case of a poor man, I do not complain of those I have had to bear. That which might, perhaps, be somewhat vexatious at the time has long ceased to be so; and I will not inflict upon the reader a statement of matters about which I seldom think, or which, if I remember them, seem but trifles.

There are, however, one or two little incidents which, as they may perhaps be admonitory to some reader who is contemplating authorship, I will briefly note. They will show that even the small amount of fame which falls to the share of such authors as myself is subjected to somewhat heavy drawbacks.

In the first instance, I was told that it had been decided in a company at Paris that my little book could not have been written by a working man. Since then I have heard that the manuscript was in so confused and imperfect a state when it passed into the publisher's hands, as to require to be almost entirely re-written by a competent person before it could be sent to the printer. Further, I have been admonished that my attention to literature had an unpropitious influence upon my tailoring business, since it was believed by many that the two pursuits were so incompatible, that if a man made any good progress in the one, he must of necessity neglect the other. By the way, I observe that these good people have no notion whatever that there is any incompatibility between habits of intemperate eating, drinking, or smoking, and a due regard to matters of business. In excuse for these habits they will maintain that every one requires some recreation or amusement, but they will not admit this excuse in my case, because they are unable to perceive that any amusement could be derived from either reading or composing a book. Time was when I should have taken the trouble of defending myself, and of attempting to show how greatly I had been enabled to make my amusements conducive to the support and well-being of myself and family. I should also have made it known that, for the most part, I attended to my literary business when I was unable, through bodily disorder, to work at my proper calling, and that I was sometimes obliged to employ one of my sons as my secretary, in consequence of my being unequal to the manual labour of writing; but having been taught the utter uselessness of arguing against foregone conclusions, and, moreover, bearing in mind the well-known Hudibrastic couplet—

> "Convince a man against his will,
> He's of the same opinion still"—

I have long ceased to make any defence against these or similar charges, and have noticed them here for the purpose of amusing the reader, rather than of giving vent to any personal feelings.

I will now record an incident, in which, however, I was very slightly concerned, and not at all with my own consent. Should it be the means of restraining some embryo author from acting rashly or unreasonably, it will not have been uselessly chronicled.

What I am about to narrate refers to one for whom I can find no more significant title than that of

THE SELF-RELYING AUTHOR.

This was a simple-minded man who took up the notion, which no persuasions could induce him to throw aside, that he was a poet, and one moreover of no mean order. His poetical theory was that which is so commonly held, namely, that whatever is written in rhyme is poetry; and that if it be of a strictly moral character it is good poetry. As this good man found each of these characteristics in his compositions, he was led to believe that he was entitled to hold the rank of an authorised poetical writer. He was, like myself, employed in a sedentary occupation, and worked at home. As his "better half" was generally absent, her occupation being that of a nurse, he was much alone, and thus had abundant opportunity for cogitation, and, very naturally, endeavoured to put his thoughts into an orderly shape. As no form seemed to be so suitable as that of verse, he adopted it, and went manfully to work, persevering until he had composed as many pieces in rhyme as would make a small volume. The question with him now was, how he could give his compositions to the public, so as to gain both fame and money by the venture. He was led to this consideration chiefly from having heard that I had published a little book, which had proved a very profitable speculation. From these shadowy materials his imagination soon formed such a glowing picture of the advantages connected with authorship, as led him to resolve upon immediately preparing his manuscript for the press. Here, however, he began to perceive that there were some difficulties to be encountered, for which he was not fully prepared. With a view to obtaining assistance in the matter, he repeatedly craved the loan of a copy of my little volume; but as it seemed to me somewhat unreasonable to be asked to lend a book to one who was well able to buy it,

I declined to grant his request.* In this dilemma he betook himself to a kindhearted lady, who was able to give him both advice and assistance. I know not how far these were bestowed, but, if I am rightly informed, they were thrown away; for the author was determined that his manuscript should go to the printer, and accordingly to the printer it went. Then, however, arose another question far more puzzling than any that had preceded it: this had special reference to the ways and means; for the printer, like a prudent tradesman, hesitated about going to work until he had some satisfactory prospects of being remunerated. After a little consideration, the author hit upon a plan which promised to relieve him of all anxiety on this head. He was the owner of several neat and pretty cottages; and it occurred to him that the required amount might be raised by mortgaging one or more of these, which he soon resolved to do; his resolution was quickly carried into effect, and the money thus provided was devoted to the payment of the printer. Whether, or not, the sale of his book enabled him to redeem his mortgaged property, I cannot say; but I think it more than

* This was not the only instance in which I was asked to lend a copy of my book. One applicant gave as a reason for making this out-of-the-way request, that it was desirable to look through the book before buying it, in order to see whether its contents would be satisfactory.

probable that it did not, especially as he employed none of the usual means of making a book known. However this may be, I have little doubt that the property was, ere long, again in his possession; inasmuch as he was of very frugal habits, and had no family to provide for; while, as in many other instances (not excepting my own), "the grey mare was the better horse." I have quite as little doubt, also, of the success of the poet in finding purchasers of his books; for, like Peter Pindar's razor-seller (of famous memory), he firmly believed that what was made in order to be sold ought not to remain unsold; and therefore he adopted all the means within his knowledge or contrivance for the purpose of disposing of his stock. Not being troubled with the sensitiveness, or delicacy of feeling common to authors, he made no difficulty of commending his literary ware; and he did so with about the same earnestness and assurance that he would have manifested had he been selling shoes. He could do this with the more freedom, because the good people among whom he chiefly looked for customers were quite unconscious that what he did was in any respect unseemly. I must (in common fairness) add, that I believe his verses to have been better adapted for usefulness, in the case of these worthy but untaught people, than would have been poetry of a higher order. In regard to the purity of its morals, he was certainly quite right when he described his book as being "a good article" and "well worth the price" put upon it. There was, of course, a slow sale; but this was, to him, an advantage rather than otherwise; for it required an additional number of excursions in order to obtain customers. The good man, although not indolent, was far from resembling him of whom it is recorded that

"Ease was his chief disease,"

and thus he was quite likely to prefer a quiet and leisurely country walk, with the accompaniment of a little pleasant gossip, to being shut up within doors, the occupant of a shoemaker's stall. Acting in accordance with these views, he was often to be seen during the fine summer mornings setting out on these expeditions. It was truly pleasant to look at him—a small, active man, neatly attired, with a countenance betokening that he was at peace with himself and with every one else. Carrying his bag of books, he wended his way with a light heart and sprightly step, while, often,

"As he went some merry lay he sang."

I know not whether he is still in this life, but think it very probable; for a heart so free from "carking care" is highly favourable to health and length of days.

I must now turn from this good man; and in doing so will take occasion to observe, that his example in regard to the manner of providing money for the printer is not intended to be held up as worthy of imitation. It is the spirit of calm and settled resolve, carrying out its purposes amidst many obstacles, that is here meant to be commended. It will be well if the example here given be followed by any one who may need to be told that without much of this spirit no one can reasonably expect to obtain the objects of his wishes, however needful they may be to his welfare.

CHAPTER VII.

I ONCE more return to my narrative, from which I have perhaps too far wandered. In the concluding sentence of the 'Memoirs of a Working Man,' I informed the reader that I had resolved to begin another literary task; and I kept my word, as I forthwith set about one which had long been in abeyance. Whether or not it will ever be completed, and, if completed, put into print, are questions which I cannot answer. The subject is one that is to me especially attractive, but I fear that it exceeds my power to do it full justice; while, even were this difficulty removed, I should be little inclined to publish what, most probably, would find but small favour with the reading public. I am therefore contented with having written what has been commended by several gentlemen who are fully competent to give a just opinion, and sometimes derive satisfaction from the thought that it may, at a future time, be useful to one member or another of my family. It is for similar reasons that I do not again try my hand at another favourite subject; for, although my first effort in that direction was greatly successful, I was indebted for that success to the efforts of several benevolent gentlemen who kindly assisted me in procuring subscribers for my intended publication, as some of them also did in the sale of the copies which remained after the subscribers had been supplied. At the present time, however, I could not expect similar aid, as all but one of these gentlemen have gone hence, while the survivor is no longer able to make such exertions. The manner of publishing these projected compositions must therefore remain for future consideration; meanwhile I think it probable that I shall, as I may find opportunity, go on with the work of preparing them for the press.

Thus much will suffice for an account of my literary performances and projects during the year 1845. I will now mention what I then did in the way of reading. I had little time or strength for this purpose; yet I looked through several interesting books, among which was a copy of Tasso's 'Jerusalem Delivered,' translated by Fairfax. I had previously read Hoole's translation of this poem, with which I was well pleased, but I was yet more gratified with that of Fairfax: this, however, was caused solely by my partiality for the structure of the verse adopted in this translation over that employed by Hoole. It may be well to add that I could give no opinion respecting the merits of the respective translations, being neither a judge of poetry nor conversant with the Italian language.

I also looked through St. Augustine's 'Confessions,' a book which I should like to read attentively, inasmuch as it gives a view of the inner life of a very remarkable man. Besides these books, I went through an essay on ' The Habitual Exercise of Love to God,' by that eminently good man the late Mr. J. J. Gurney. I venture to recommend this little book to the attention of all who wish to learn the way to genuine happiness; for therein it is made evident that true happiness may be enjoyed

"Even in this noisy, this unsettled scene."

In addition to these books I had, by the favour of an honoured friend, an opportunity of reading a work which could not but be deeply interesting to an invalid like myself. This was a treatise on 'The Power of the Soul over the Body.' I will not presume to give anything like a critical opinion of this work; but I am, nevertheless, at liberty to state that I believe it to be of great worth, as it reached a fourth edition in less than four years from the date of its first publication. It is worthy of remark that its author is himself a striking example of the "power" concerning which he has written—having long been the subject of severe and almost unmitigated bodily disorder.

Here I close my notices of the year 1845: a year during which I was often, and in various ways, reminded of that quaintly-worded but finely expressive proverb already quoted,* " God's providence is my inheritance ;" and I take pleasure in recording my full belief in its truthfulness as applied to myself and my family.

In entering upon another year's history, I again advertise the reader that it will comprise but little of an amusing character; if, however, it should contain what may subserve the higher purposes of instruction or admonition, I shall be far more satisfied than I should be if it were entirely made up of merely entertaining materials. At the beginning of this year my usual half-solitary state was made yet more lonely by reason of several changes in my domestic circumstances, which, as they could not be interesting to the reader, I shall forbear to dwell upon. Thus I was led to look about me, in order to find something wherewith to entertain myself when for the time I might be free from my usual duties. It had been utter folly to have attempted engaging in out-of-door amusements; while it would have been quite idle to have looked for any visitors in whose conversation I could feel an interest; I therefore had no alternative but that of endeavouring to find entertainment in what was near at hand, and which might be suggestive of pleasant ideas or recollections. Being in earnest, I had the reward usually given to earnestness of effort, for I suc-

* At page 19.

ceeded in finding an object which suited my wishes. This was a copy of that volume which, for its unapproachable excellence, well deserves its distinctive title of 'The Book.' Although much worn, and somewhat mutilated, yet it pleased and still pleases me more than could any other copy, for it was the chosen companion of my early years, and therefore serves to remind me of much that either amuses the fancy or touches the heart.

The reader will perhaps bear with me while I give some description of this antiquated volume. Its cover is of wood, overlaid with leather, which is ornamented and defended by pieces of brass-work, and it still retains portions of the clasps which formerly secured it. From the appearance of the edges, I conclude that they were originally gilt. Thus much for its exterior; internally it presents several features which do not appear in modern editions of the book: first, there is a copy (in the old English character) of the Royal Proclamation for the 'Uniformity of Common Prayer:' then follows a Preface, and this is succeeded by an article upon 'Ceremonies:' then comes the 'Book of Common Prayer,' bearing date in the reign of King Charles I. The several books are embellished (?) by ornamented initial letters and tail-pieces, some of the latter appearing to be emblematical. The Apocryphal books are included, and occupy their usual places. I take pleasure in noting these little particulars; but I feel a much higher pleasure in telling the reader that the book bears indubitable marks of having been much and carefully read; some portions have, in consequence, become a good deal worn, especially the Book of Psalms. Here many leaves which had given way have been carefully replaced—by one, however, who seems either to have had no knowledge of numerical signs, or to have thought that, so long as the loose leaves were again secured, it mattered not where they were placed. Hence, what remains of the book is now in a state of most admirable disorder, requiring no little trouble to be read consecutively; and, after all the care that has been taken, the psalms now remaining do not amount to more than ninety-six out of the hundred and fifty which compose the book.

I love, in imagination, to look back upon the circumstances under which I was wont to peruse this venerable volume. My readings were chiefly by stealth; for often when I was supposed to be asleep I was thus employed by the feeble light of a rush candle, and the marks are still remaining which I made with a pencil of my own manufacture, in order to note where I left off reading. From that time to the present, the book has seldom, if ever, been read by any one except myself; and therefore it is not much more worn than it was nearly half a century ago. I continue to use it, in spite of its small and in many places almost illegible type, although I am now unable to read a well-printed book without the aid of spectacles.

How it came into the hands of my grandmother, to whom it belonged, I know not; but it could not have been by purchase, except at second or third hand, for, in its original state, it must have borne a much higher price than any poor person could have afforded to give. I have often employed my fancy in conjecturing what might have been the circumstances and the religious habits of its earlier owners, and thus I sometimes form an ideal picture which it gives me much pleasure to contemplate. For example, I seem to behold the interior of a lowly yet neat and comfortable cottage: the time is Sunday evening; an aged man and woman are respectively engaged, the one in reading, the other in hearing read, some portion of this volume—most likely the chapters which formed the lessons for the day's Church-service, or that chapter which contains the text of the minister's sermon. They give good token of being deeply interested with what the book announces, and, moreover, that they are deriving from it much of that inward peace which too often is unknown to the learned and critical reader of Holy Writ. With but little trouble I can further picture to myself this venerable couple, in the attitude of worship, giving utterance to their devout feelings in the beautiful language of the devotional compositions which the piety of learned and eloquent men has provided for the use and benefit of their unlettered brethren; or, I can imagine a lonely man or woman similarly engaged. Perhaps the solitary reader may have been bereft of a conjugal partner, and looks here for words of comfort and encouragement, such as may inspire the heart with that mingled fortitude and resignation which nothing but a full belief in the declarations of this book can be the means of producing—for here alone are "life and immortality brought to light."

Now, are not these delightful imaginings? Do they not far surpass, in their power to give true pleasure, all the gaudy spectacles or the most fascinating day-dreams with which multitudes attempt to amuse the imagination or to satisfy the heart's intense yearnings after rest and peace? I leave the reader to make such answer as may be the most in agreement either with his personal experience or the testimony of existing facts.

As the greater number of my few books were given to me by justly-esteemed friends, some of whom have since gone into the world of spirits, there is further scope for my imagination to employ itself in drawing pictures resembling that which I have above given. Not unfrequently do I allow it to take that course, and find that it brings me an amount of pleasurable feeling which I should in vain look for from external objects.

But I must not enlarge upon this subject. What

I have said is sufficient to show how a state of seclusion, or even of solitude, may be made to wear a cheerful if not an inviting aspect, and thus become, not merely tolerable, but genuinely happy. It were easy to prove that almost every other object within my view has a similar power of exciting the imaginative faculty, and thereby of becoming the instrument of instructing the mind or usefully affecting the heart. The thoughtful reader will not, however, require to be told how these effects may be produced, while the unthinking one will not be likely to give any serious attention to such a topic. I therefore leave it, and pass on to other matters.

The next which I shall notice is connected with a particular day in the month of February. Some years ago, on the sixteenth of that month, I heard, for the first time in the season, the song of the thrush. It would be impossible for me to listen to the early song of this bird without being conscious of emotions which I cannot adequately describe. Sometimes they are altogether of a cheerful kind, while at others they are dashed with melancholy. In either case, however, they are feelings that I love to cherish, and of which I hope never to be unsusceptible. On the occasion referred to, the notes of this bird struck me as being what our great epic poet affirms of the nightingale's—" most musical, most melancholy." Yet the melancholy was of that character which one feels disposed to cherish rather than to deprecate, especially when in a languid physical state, such as that under the influence of which I wrote the following lines:—

> Lighthearted herald of the coming spring!
>   To fancy's ear thy wildly warbling strains
>   Speak of fresh foliage, emerald-tinted plains,
> And flowers that all around sweet odours fling.
> Of these, yea more than these, thy glad notes bring
>   Fair promise, for they tell of azure skies,
>   Bright days, soft breezes, and the melodies
> Of birds, and rills, and insect's tremulous wing.
> To him whose healthful frame and gladsome breast
>   Are yet unscath'd by withering care or pain,
>   Thy chanting seems to say that he again
> Shall be with vernal joys and pleasures blest:
> But to the victim of disease, or grief,
> Thy spirit-soothing tale brings small relief!

This little piece found its way into a literary journal, then in course of weekly publication. In giving it here I am guiltless of piracy, inasmuch as it brought no " grist to the mill;" in plain English, it was not paid for. I am therefore free to use it, but, in doing so, have to beg that the reader will not for a moment imagine that I presume to regard myself as a poet. I make no claim whatever to this high character, and therefore feel that I may fairly be spared the castigation with which poetasters and rhymesters are sometimes visited.

In the spring-time of this year I was bereft by death of another patron. This was a gentleman to whom I had been indebted for much courteous attention. He was on his way to a far-distant country, but before he had nearly completed his voyage thither, that of his earthly life terminated. His body was committed to the custody of the great deep, and probably ere now has been resolved into its primitive elements. When thinking of him, I am sometimes reminded of that touching passage in Milton's 'Lycidas'—

> "To interpose a little ease,
> Let our frail thoughts dally with false surmise,
> Ah, me! whilst thee the shores and sounding seas
> Wash far away, where'er thy bones are hurl'd,
> Whether beyond the stormy Hebrides,
> Where thou, perhaps, under the whelming tide
> Visit'st the bottom of the monstrous world;
> Or whether thou, to our moist vows denied,
> Sleep'st by the fable of Bellerus old,
> Where the great vision of the guarded mount
> Looks tow'rd Namancos and Bayona's hold;
> Look homeward, angel, now, and melt with ruth,
> And, O ye dolphins, waft the hapless youth."

This, in my opinion, is a passage of surpassing beauty; but if the poet had not gone beyond this point,—if he had contented himself, as so many poets have done, with conducting the departed spirit no farther than to the gate of the invisible world,—I should have been far less charmed by either the elegance or the pathos of his verses. Milton, however, was neither disinclined nor afraid to pass the

> "Bounds of place and time."

He therefore follows his yet beloved friend, enters into the " Eternal City " (rightly so called), and there discerns that friend, participating in the felicity enjoyed by the "spirits of just men made perfect." Animated by the glorious vision, he describes it in a manner equally worthy of the enlightened Christian and the transcendent poet.

Considering that poetry had its origin in heaven, and that the true poet is also a prophet; remembering also its powerful influence upon the human mind and heart, it is to be regretted that so few of those who are masters in that " divine art " should aspire to the full dignity of their high calling, by becoming the teachers of a " divine philosophy "— a philosophy which inculcates the doctrine that all who " walk with God " while here, shall find what is called death to be but the beginning of an immortal and blissful life.

There is great need that every possible effort should be made to counteract the baneful influence of that worldliness of spirit which is so generally prevalent. It is freely admitted that the Christian minister is specially charged with the " cure of souls;" yet, as there are multitudes who will not receive his ministrations, it is the duty of all whom they are willing to hear to aim at promoting their moral improvement. Among these there is perhaps none who is so likely to be an approved teacher as the genuine poet. Every one, therefore, who sustains this high character should aim to be a teacher of spiritual and eternal truths, remembering, for his encouragement, that

> "A verse may catch him who a sermon flies,
> And turn delight into a sacrifice."

Of these truths none can be more worthy of especial attention than the doctrine of a future and endless life—a doctrine concerning which there exists a lamentable amount of mingled ignorance, indifference, and error. That this is an evil of no trifling moment is evident from the fact that, without a full, cordial, and enlightened belief in this doctrine, there can be no foundation for either genuine morality or true religion.

At the hazard of seeming harsh, I feel impelled to state my opinion—an opinion not hastily formed—that a full and consistent belief in this doctrine is comparatively rare; otherwise I cannot account for many allowed, if not cherished, principles and practices which are wholly inconsistent with any reasonable hope of a blessed immortality. But here I must check myself; "I speak as to wise men;" let them "judge what I say."

I now come again to my story. It was, if I rightly remember, in this year (1846) that I was favoured with the loan of two books which I found to be not a little interesting. These were Mr. Macaulay's 'Lays of Ancient Rome,' and Mr.

Carlyle's 'Sartor Resartus.' Of either of these works it would be unseemly in me to attempt to give a critical opinion; but I may be allowed to observe, respecting Mr. Carlyle's volume, that while I regard it as very entertaining, I have much doubt as to its useful tendency. Indeed, I cannot help thinking that the author has shown here, as in others of his works, that he is far more powerful in the work of shaking or pulling down than in that of strengthening or building up. Any system of either morals or religion that shall promise to be of real value, is not, I fear, to be looked for from this gifted but eccentric writer.

Leaving this subject, however, as beyond my province, I have to notice what more nearly concerns myself, and which I hope may be more useful to some of my readers. About this time I was put under a new course of medical treatment, more, however, by way of experiment than from the hope of my deriving much benefit from the change. A long-standing disorder, such as mine, was likely to resist all attempts, of whatever kind, to treat it successfully; yet I thought it my duty to try what effect would be produced by the homœopathic system. This I resolved upon in consequence of advice given me by a gentleman who has long watched over my health with unwearied care, his only recompense having been the "testimony of a good conscience," and to whose judicious treatment I believe I am indebted for exemption from many of the severer inconveniences attendant upon my disorder.

This gentleman, having seen the effects of homœopathy upon the patients of a brother physician, was induced to advise me to make trial of it. I followed this advice, being careful, as is my invariable practice in such matters, to act in strict accordance with the prescribed rules. I continued under this treatment for about a year, when circumstances arose which obliged me to forego it. From that time I have totally abstained from medicine, and therefore, perhaps, am the better able to judge how far I was relieved by the homœopathic treatment. Of course I give no opinion concerning the comparative merits of this and the allopathic system : all that I have to do is to state its effects in my own case, which I believe to have been beneficial, and that to a greater extent than I could reasonably have expected. Perhaps I shall not go beyond my proper limits if I remark that the very minute doses of medicine prescribed by this mode of treatment, and which have caused so much sarcasm in some quarters and pleasantry in others, seem to suit my case better than the larger doses given under the old system. As to their being really powerful I can have no doubt, for I was made conscious of this by symptoms which, considering my long-continued use of medicine, I could not well mistake. If I were again to place myself under medical treatment, it should, if possible, be the homœopathic.

In dismissing this subject I may remark that the exact and discriminating rules of homœopathy respecting diet strike me as being very judicious. If they be duly observed they can hardly fail of being highly useful assistants to the medicine. In general there is too little regard paid by sick people to the important matter of a suitable regimen; and it is, I think, to this neglect that much of the alleged failure of medicine is to be ascribed. It must be obvious to every reflecting person that neither the skill of the physician nor the virtue of drugs can greatly avail where the patient neither takes care to regulate his diet in a suitable manner nor to exercise in other respects a proper degree of self-control. It should moreover be remembered that the careless or unruly patient is quite as unkind to himself as he is unjust to others by the neglect of due watchfulness and precaution in regard to what none but himself can possibly regulate.

CHAPTER VIII.

I have stated that I no longer make use of medicine, but I omitted to add that I continue to use stramonium, by smoking it, when my respiration is difficult.

Although not conversant with botanical science, I have some knowledge of this plant, which perhaps may prove useful to some one or other of my readers, and not the less so from my having been forced to learn it. The scientific name of this plant is "Datura stramonium," which I cannot translate. Its common name is "thorn-apple;" in some parts of the country, however, it is called "fire-apple." It is, in my judgment, worthy to be called beautiful. In a strong, rich soil it will sometimes attain the height of nearly three feet. The leaves are large, formed of three parts, with jagged edges, and are of a darkish green colour. It commonly flowers in July; the flower is white and cup-shaped. Its seed-vessel is an oval-shaped pod, covered with strong and sharply-pointed prickles, and divided into many compartments, each of which is filled with seeds, which, when ripe, are of a dark brown colour, in size and shape resembling tare-seed. The proper time for gathering it is when the leaves are full-grown, which is when the flower is going off. The only really useful parts are the leaves and the leaf-stalks; all the fibrous or woody parts I find to be rather injurious than useful. The proper manner of curing it is by drying it in the open air, but it must not be exposed to either the sun or the rain. When sufficiently dry it should be put into a paper bag to keep it free from dust and other impurities. In smoking it care should be taken to swallow the spittle, and also, as far as possible, the smoke. It should be used only when the breathing is so difficult as to be painfully inconvenient, and should be put aside as soon as relief has been obtained, which, if it does not yield speedily, it is probable that no good will result from continuing its use. It may, indeed, as I have learned by my own experience, be rather hurtful than beneficial, and therefore should for the time be discontinued. Any asthmatic person who possesses the means will do well to cultivate this plant, as he will thereby insure its genuineness, and also, if due care be taken in curing and packing it, its freedom from mould or dust. Much additional suffering is sometimes endured by the patient through the admixture of other substances with the stramonium.

I have been thus circumstantial and exact in my directions, because I know from painful experience the distressing nature of the very unmanageable disorder referred to; and, moreover, how greatly its severity may be increased by the want of knowledge or caution. I earnestly hope that what has been stated may be the means of preserving some asthmatic patient from the more violent attacks of his distressing complaint. In what follows he will, I believe, find some hints which, if acted on, may further promote his ease.

Every one must be aware that habits are readily formed, when they respect such things as are either pleasing or convenient, but every one is not equally aware that they may be almost as easily adopted in regard to what at first is uninviting, if not indeed positively disagreeable. It is thus even with medicine, as I learned through the medium of much inconvenience. From similar inconvenience I would fain be helpful in guarding my fellow-patients, and am, therefore, induced to warn them against all medicines, except when plainly needful, as their frequent and regular use will probably ere long become a fixed habit, and this in its turn will soon render it necessary to increase the quantity. Thus the habit becomes the cause of the necessity, while the necessity of course serves to strengthen and confirm the habit. It was in this way that I brought upon myself a good deal of additional trouble. I was led to use ipecacuanha in small but frequently repeated doses, with a view to promote a free expectoration, and thus to moderate the difficulty of breathing. Soon, however, I was compelled to a more frequent repetition of the dose in order to produce the desired effect, and the issue was that my respiration became so unsteady as to make it almost impossible to keep it in any tolerable order. In addition to this serious inconvenience I incurred one that was yet more adverse, not to my comfort merely, but moreover to my interests, for I became much reduced in bodily strength, and thus was made more liable to severe fits of asthma. I, therefore, earnestly advise that this course should be carefully avoided or abandoned. When I discovered what mischief I had been doing by following such a course, I resolved to forsake it, and I did so immediately. In carrying out this resolution I had full proof of the power which long-continued habit acquires over us, for, during a considerable time after I had ceased to use the medicine, I felt the need of it at the usual hour. I was not, however, to be moved from my purpose, and in the end was rewarded by being freed from the necessity, as well as from the habit.

In like manner, the frequent and long-continued use of stramonium eventually produced a necessity for it, which at length became so unremitting and pressing as greatly to interfere with my power of sleeping. For not fewer than twelve or thirteen years I have been forced to have recourse to it upon an average more than once in an hour. I have long been unable to sleep during two consecutive hours, as at the expiration of less than that time the lungs become so much in want of their usual quietus as to waken me. Whether or not I shall ever be able to refrain even in part from the use of this palliative, I cannot determine; but hitherto my efforts in that direction have been unsuccessful. That the necessity in this case is a real one I cannot doubt; but I nevertheless believe that this necessity was produced by a previous habit of resorting to the herb more frequently than was absolutely needful. There is, however, one encouraging circumstance in connection with my present use of stramonium, namely, that I now get the required relief much sooner than formerly, about a minute's smoking being in general sufficient for my purpose. This seems to indicate that I may yet be enabled to get the mastery over what has for so long a time held me in thraldom.

Passing from matters personal to myself, I will notice the case of a former fellow-workman, who was the unwilling slave of opium-eating. He had been induced to resort to this deleterious drug in order to obtain relief from the acute pain of a disease to which he was subject; and as this was of long duration, he continued the use of opium until, as in my case, a necessity arose for larger doses. Thus he went on gradually increasing the quantity, until he became, as I have said, a slave to the pernicious practice, which I believe he would gladly have renounced, both on account of its expensiveness and its very injurious influence upon his health, but the habit was too strongly confirmed; it had indeed become a stern necessity. Without this auxiliary he was spiritless and deficient in the necessary strength for following his employment; whereas, when under its exciting influence, he was exceedingly cheerful, and would at times get through an amount of work nearly equal to that of two men. Meanwhile, his appetite failing, he ate less and less and gradually became greatly emaciated, his whole appearance betokening disease and decay. In the very prime of his years he fell a victim to this baneful, yet, in his case, unavoidable habit. Death seized upon him, and he was no more seen.

Here I seem to be justified in making a few remarks upon the duty of avoiding the formation of any habit that may be likely to have an ill effect upon either the body or the mind. Whatever only *seems* to have such a tendency should be most carefully shunned, for when it is once confirmed there is great difficulty in abandoning it, however imprudent or vicious it may be. I have seen many striking examples of the misery and ruin consequent upon foolish or immoral habits. One of the most impressive of these was in the case of a young man whom I warned against confirming himself in practices which then he had but recently adopted. He took my warning in good part, but neglected to act upon it. We parted, and I saw him no more until after he had sacrificed health and vigour, and was rapidly approaching the end of his earthly course. He then saw his folly, but it was too late. I will not attempt to describe the feeling with which I heard him express his regret that he had not been wise enough to avoid the habits by which in early life he became the victim of a fatal disease.

To this instance I could add many others of equally painful interest, but I forbear, and will only observe that the descent into the depths of folly or wickedness is comparatively easy, while the return thence is a work of such difficulty as to have mastered the powers of a multitude which could not be quickly numbered. Who can reckon up the victims that have immolated themselves upon the altars of gluttony, drunkenness, and lasciviousness? They have indeed been multitudinous, while every successive day adds to their numbers. Among the most pernicious of evil habits is that of using stimulants in the shape of either strong drinks or baneful drugs. I would not wilfully undervalue or decry what has been effected by temperance societies, but I am fearful that ardent spirits have in many instances been abandoned to no good purpose, having only given place to other means of producing intoxication. My fear arises from the fact of the vastly increased importation of opium which has been going on during the last five or six years. There is full proof that this increased supply is the result of an increased demand, that demand being for the purpose of home consumption.

It is a truth not sufficiently recognised that the habitual use, by an individual, of this or any other drug or medicament, for the mere purpose of exhilarating the animal spirits, constitutes him a drunkard, although he may totally abstain from the more commonly-used intoxicating liquors. That this drunkenness is of a more thoroughly degrading and demoralising character than that which is produced by any other means is a fact which admits of no successful contradiction.

But I will not enlarge upon a subject concerning which I can hardly give an opinion without seeming to be either hostile or indifferent to what is called "the temperance movement." This movement has my best wishes, and I honour those who are engaged in it; but I am free to confess that my faith in its utility is far from being strong. Neither the effects hitherto produced by it, nor the still increasing consumption of "fire-water," seem to warrant the conclusion that much good is likely to be effected by this means. It were better, I think, that people should be temperate from the influence of a directly religious principle than by means of either verbal or written pledges to that effect.

In passing, I would observe that a good cause may easily be damaged by unworthy friends or by an injudicious management. That the temperance movement has suffered from each of these sources I have no doubt, but I must not here set down the instances to which I refer. What I now have to notice has reference to another subject, which in part has been suggested by what I have said concerning the force of habit. I here allude to the power which, in some instances, the physical constitution possesses of successfully resisting the adverse influences of circumstances and practices which usually are highly prejudicial to health, if not indeed destructive of life. I have known several instances of this power, one of which is so truly remarkable as to induce me to relate it somewhat particularly; and I can vouch for the truthfulness of all that I may record concerning the person referred to. The reader may, if he pleases, call my narrative

THE HISTORY OF A HERMIT.

This was a man who, in early life, took part in the busy scenes of the world. His father was the landlord of a public-house, and employed him in the business. While yet a young man he cultivated on his own account a small garden, in which he reared for sale both fruit and vegetables. What follows shows that he was even then a shrewd and prudent business man. On Sunday evenings his garden was open to visitors, who, on paying a small sum for admission, were allowed to walk in it, and to gather fruit at pleasure. For those who preferred the fruit without the trouble of gathering it he provided a sufficient quantity, which was at their service on paying a small additional sum. What remained after he had sold all that he could in this way was made into wine, and brought out for sale in the following year. After some time he succeeded his father in the alehouse, but still continued to cultivate his garden. He did not, however, long remain a publican; but, procuring some additional ground, he built thereon a dwelling-house. Afterwards he took more ground, and, turning his former garden into an orchard, commenced business as a nurseryman. As a few years after this there arose in his neighbourhood a great demand for young trees and shrubs, he found it a very profitable speculation, a high price being readily obtained.

About this time he joined a religious community, and bore some part in its devotional services; but his manner and language were marked by much oddity, so that he was rather discouraged by his associates. Subsequently he joined that nondescript body which the most eloquent of modern divines has characterised as "the thick-skinned monster of the ooze and mire, which no weapon can pierce, no discipline can tame." Soon, however, he left this sect, and refrained from joining any other, thus preparing the way for the state of solitude upon which he was shortly to enter. When he had made up his mind as to his future mode of life, his manners became so unpleasing that his wife and children were constrained to leave him, and they took up their abode in the house which he had formerly built, which, as it was too chargeable to be rented by a labouring man, and badly situated for those who could afford the expense of holding it, had long been without an occupant. He was now quite alone, and thus was free to give way to all the strange fancies in which he might choose to indulge. It appears that he had resolved on becoming a hermit for the term of seven years, and, further, to observe the following rather stringent rules :—First, to work in all kinds of weather ; secondly, to make no distinction of days ; thirdly, never to shave himself or trim the hair of his head ; fourthly, to eat nothing but bread and to drink nothing but water. His bread was supplied to him by his wife at fixed times and in given quantities, while his pump afforded him all the water that he needed for drinking. As to washing himself, this does not appear to have formed any part of the discipline prescribed by his vow, and consequently he was not a little grimed with dirt. He was also very ragged, as he did not allow himself any new apparel. He had, when I saw him, such a huge mass of hair upon his head as to prevent its shape from being clearly visible, while his beard was of great thickness and of a most venerable length. Through his excessive quantity of hair it was difficult to see his eyes, while his other features were yet more closely concealed. Altogether he was a strange-looking person. He was calm in his demeanour, and conversed rationally enough, except when he adverted to religious matters, upon which he was very wild and incoherent.

During the whole time of his seclusion he seldom went outside of his ground, except for the purpose of learning what orders had been left for trees or shrubs with a person whom he had deputed to receive them, and who lived close at hand. These visits were made under cover of the twilight; and on the next day he employed himself in getting ready whatever might have been ordered. In this business he met with no hindrances from the weather, inasmuch as he rigidly adhered to his rule of working, whatever might be its state. However wet his clothes, they were never changed, nor were they dried otherwise than by the sun or air, or by the warmth of his own person. If, while at work, he wished for a little rest, he took it upon the ground where he was then standing, utterly regardless of its being either damp or muddy. He was equally careless of either wind, rain, or snow. Thus he went on for seven years, retaining his full health and vigour during the whole time. At the termination of this period he relaxed a little in the severity of his rules; but this indulgence did not go so far as to allow of his returning to his wife and children: it amounted only to going, in the afternoon, to take a cup of tea with his aged mother, and to warm himself at her fire; for, as it would seem, he did not allow himself that luxury in his hermitage. He continued this practice for about three years longer, at the close of which (his vow being fully accomplished) he went home, and thenceforth lived with his wife and children. He now trimmed, or rather thinned, the hair of his head and beard, and put himself into decent clothing.

After some time he came into possession of a small farm, on which he sold his grounds and tenement, and went to live in the farm-house; but, with the exception of taking his meals with his family, and sometimes trimming his head and beard, he made no change in his habits. As he did not care about dressing decently, he soon became very shabby, and moreover very dirty—so dirty, indeed, as to be disgusting to his wife and children; while a little grandchild refused to acknowledge him as her grandfather, and would call him by no other name than that of "The Old Man." He still continued to work in all sorts of weather, observing, on being advised to leave off when the rain was falling heavily, that one kind of weather ought to be taken with another. He was seen, while tending some swine that were feeding, stretched upon the wet and dirty ground, and seemingly with perfect satisfaction. At a contested election, some few years ago, he was prevailed upon to go to the voting-place, where, although he had been a little prepared for the occasion, he excited considerable pleasantry by his grotesque appearance. He is now quite infirm, but this would seem to be solely by reason of old age, for he has never been in ill health, nor does he even now show any symptoms of bodily ailment.

The history of this eccentric man is, I think, sufficiently curious and instructive to warrant my having so long dwelt upon it. It is remarkable as giving an example of the power which the body may acquire of enduring hardships by means of regular and persevering habits. As to the cause which produced the eccentricity referred to, it is not possible for me to explain it, but I do not think it was mental weakness, or, to any considerable extent, derangement; and I come to this conclusion from his having been remarkable for the judicious manner in which he managed his business and all other affairs, as also for his correctness in keeping and settling his accounts. To his honour be it remarked, that he was believed to be fully as careful not to wrong his customers as he was not to suffer himself to be wronged. It is much to be wished that his strictly upright manner of dealing were more generally followed; and I recommend his example in this respect to such of my readers as may be engaged or are about to engage in business. The remembrance of it may perhaps guard them against being led into practices which, although often attempted to be justified on the ground of their being very common, are of a highly disreputable character. I forbear to point them out further than by observing, that whatever is done in order to make a profit by other than fair and honourable means must be classed among them.

This leads me to notice the practice, so common among magazine and newspaper proprietors, of publishing advertisements without any regard to their moral tendency. I have been repeatedly grieved by hearing what has been said in justification of this very reprehensible practice, by men from whom I was warranted in looking for better things. Their excuse is either the same as that above named, or that the money derived from this source is necessary to the support of their publication; and these unworthy reasons are allowed to govern the conduct of men who are specially bound to act in agreement with the strictest rules of Christian morality; I am bold to say that if a professedly moral or religious journal cannot be duly supported without the money derivable from these discreditable sources, it ought to be discontinued. There is no alternative between this and a rigid exclusion of everything that may be of a doubtful moral tendency.

Dismissing this subject, I now turn to one which, during the course of the last few years, has often been forced upon my attention. This is mendicity, which, besides being in itself a public evil, is the parent of other and greater evils. Of course I refer only to what may be called professional begging, or the mendicity of sturdy beggars. There are few people except the sufferers who are aware of the frequency and the pertinacity with which infirm persons in London are assailed by the able-bodied mendicants who infest the public thoroughfares; these beggars are not only troublesome, but are also sometimes a cause of considerable fear. I have often been assailed by them when it was evident that I could not take care of myself, and in one instance had much fear of being robbed, if not otherwise illtreated. Sometimes, however, I have succeeded in making these people instrumental in furnishing me with knowledge concerning the "art and mystery" of professional begging. By putting questions that were not of the usual kind, and which did not clearly show what I was aiming at, I have been enabled to extract such answers as I wished for, and thus I have by degrees collected a goodly amount of information which I think may fairly be deemed credible, and which at a future time may perhaps be made useful. I must not, however, allow myself now to dwell upon it, as I wish, before I pass on to other subjects, to state my opinion concerning the question of public begging. As regards really necessitous persons who are known to be of good character, I think that these ought to be allowed to beg in their respective parishes, and moreover that they should be treated in a courteous manner. Nothing should be either said or done to make them conscious of being considered as degraded beings, for there is really nothing degrading in a truly necessitous person asking for the benevolent aid of others, any more than there is in the ignorant asking for instruction, or the sick and diseased praying for medical assistance. So long as it is known that the petitioners have been unavoidably reduced to a state of want, and that what is given to them will be frugally used, I cannot but think that they should be left at full liberty to request the help of their richer brethren, who in relieving cases like these will find that the blessing promised in Holy Writ to those who consider the poor is not withheld from themselves. I am inclined to believe that a much less amount of money than that which is extorted by the huge crowd of able-bodied professional mendicants would suffice to give all needful help to the class of deserving beggars. Meanwhile all those who voluntarily live by begging should be made to forego their calling and be placed under an effective control: they should be required to work regularly and diligently, and, failing to do so, should be subjected to such correction as might be likely to bring them into orderly and industrious habits. If due attention were to be given to the matter, there could, as I believe, be full and suitable employment found for them without damaging the interests of well-deserving workpeople; and as their numbers, under a proper system of management, would be likely to undergo a gradual decrease, there would probably come a time when the community would be relieved from the burden of maintaining an army of mendicants.

Here, turning from men to books, I remember that it was in the year 1846 that I began to read that very curious work Burton's 'Anatomy of Melancholy.' I had long wished to get hold of it; but, as it was a somewhat scarce volume, I could not readily borrow it. A new edition, however, removed

H

the difficulty, as a copy then came into the hands of a friend, of whom I obtained the loan of it. I name these little matters in order to show that I do not waste any part of my small earnings in the purchase of books. My ability to read with ease having during the last three or four years been much weakened, I have not even now nearly got through my task.

Regarding this work, I am astonished at the extensive and widely varied reading of the author. I have never met with another book containing any approach to so large an amount of reference to the works of other writers; and can hardly help imagining that the author was endued with some peculiar power both of reading and recollecting.

Without intending to compare myself to this wonderful man I may observe that my own memory was formerly very retentive, not only of the general tenor of what I read or heard, but also of the exact words. Of late, however, I have been much less favoured in regard to this very valuable power, so that now I can *remember* much better than I can *recollect*.* There was, indeed, one

---

* I long imagined that remembering and recollecting were synonymous; but, eventually, was led to perceive my error by reading a passage in Cowper's letters. I cannot give the exact words, but it is to the following effect:— "My memory is not what it once was; it is far less retentive. I very soon quite forget what I have read. A bystander would, perhaps, say that this was rather an advantage than otherwise, as the books which may have been read

instance in which my power of remembering was not much better than that of my recollecting, as the following brief story will make manifest:—About three years ago I was for (I believe) the fifth time looking through Cary's translation of Dante's celebrated poem; when I found that the book seemed to be very nearly new to me, for I could not remember to have previously read more than one passage. I have never been able to account for this almost total forgetfulness of what I had repeatedly perused; I was the more puzzled because I well remembered the pleasure which it had given me whenever I had read it. I was indeed a good deal harassed at the time by many perplexing matters; but as I had often been perplexed without having been thus strangely forgetful, I could not ascribe my want of memory to this cause, and must even now leave it without being able to account for it. Some one of my readers may perhaps solve the problem, and, if so, I should be not a little pleased to know what may be his views concerning it.

This little incident leads me to make a few remarks upon the subject of memory. What I have stated in regard to the now weakened condi-

are always new; but I beg the bystander's pardon, for I can remember although I cannot recollect." Meaning that when the book was again read he was aware that he had read it before; but that he could not, without its aid, call to mind either its contents or the fact of having perused it.

tion of my retentive power must be understood as referring only to matters of comparatively recent occurrence, since in regard to whatever belongs to my earlier history I have the full power of both recollecting and remembering; I now find in this power a source of considerable advantage and pleasure, as it enables me to read without a book when I am too much worn to allow of my using one. Thus I often recall the contents of books which were the companions of my earlier years, and among them I do not forget to include those which make up the volume of Holy Writ. Of these I can recollect enough to employ all the time which I may have at my command, and I sometimes go through several chapters, together with rather long passages from the works of Thomson, Young, Cowper, and other eminent poets. Herein I find mental entertainment at all times, but especially during the otherwise tedious hours of the night when I am not permitted to

"steep my senses in forgetfulness."

I have but little respect for any artificial helps to the memory, being of opinion that it is best aided by frequent and patient exercise; yet I have for many years occasionally endeavoured to assist mine by means of a plan which, being of my own contrivance, is doubtless sufficiently clumsy. It has, however, the merit of being very simple and also of answering my purpose. I require it chiefly when I am endeavouring to recollect names, whether of persons, places, or things. The alphabet in the regular order of its letters supplies the materials; and the manner of working it is as follows: If, for example, I want to recollect the name of Smith, but cannot readily call it to mind, having however an impression of its beginning with the letter S, I take that letter and add to it one which will fairly follow it in forming a word. Of course I begin with the letter A, and go on until I come to M, when I am pretty sure of recollecting the name required. If, however, I fail to do so by this first trial, but yet believe that M is the second letter of the name, I then begin with the letters Sm, and go on as before. This seldom fails to serve my purpose; but if it should, I take the letters Sma, and add thereto another letter taken as before in regular succession; and in case of failing in my third effort (which I rarely do), I continue the experiment by using the remaining letters, until I have either succeeded, or have exhausted my stock of materials. In the latter case, however, I do not feel discouraged, for I consider that the time which has been spent in the process has neither been wasted nor unwisely used, inasmuch as I have set the retentive faculty to work, and probably have thereby imparted to it some additional vigour. Sometimes, indeed, I feel assured of this, as, not long after I have made this effort, I am suddenly supplied with what I had vainly been labouring to obtain.

I have now more frequent occasion than formerly for this aid to memory, and find it of considerable use, but I do not presume to recommend it to others, first, because of its clumsiness and tediousness, and secondly, because I believe it to be better for every one to act upon a self-contrived plan as being more likely to answer individual purposes. I do, however, seriously recommend every one whose memory seems to need assistance to adopt some means of helping it; and I repeat that I consider that plan the most efficient which consists in giving it frequent and earnest exercise. This I think can hardly fail to improve its active power. But, after all, I am not fully of opinion that a naturally bad memory is so common as it is alleged to be; my doubts upon this matter arise from the well-known fact of so few people forgetting what affects either their interests or their enjoyments. The child rarely forgets the usual time of receiving

"the biscuit or confectionary plum;"

the schoolboy forgets not that a holiday season is approaching; neither does the pleasure-seeker forget that he has heard of a new source of amusement, nor the money-hunter that he has been told of where or how he may obtain additional pelf. In short, there are but few subjects concerning which it is usual to hear any complaints of a defective power of recollection. I may not, however, omit to note, that among these is one of paramount importance to every rational human being; and this is nothing less than that of the relation in which men stand to their Creator. Here there is, indeed, a widely prevailing and a most lamentable forgetfulness—one deeply culpable, and fraught with fearful peril.

The sum of the matter seems to be this: where the affections or the worldly interests are involved, there is rarely any serious complaint made of what is rather affectedly called a " treacherous memory." It is only where the will does not consent to help the retentive faculty that this faculty seems to be faulty. It is not, however, fair to charge it with treachery, for how can it be unfaithful to that which has not been committed to its keeping?

CHAPTER IX.

Having dwelt so long upon the subject of aids to memory, I fear I may be found tedious; yet the courteous reader will perhaps bear with me while I make one or two additional remarks. First, then, if it be a duty to attempt to improve the memory wherever it seems to be defective, it is equally so to take care that, so far as may be possible, all that is evil and false be rigorously excluded therefrom. This, however, can only be done by taking care to store it with what is good and true. It is a difficult task, and perhaps one that does not admit of being fully accomplished in the present life; yet what may be done is of considerable amount; and this must not be neglected, as indeed it cannot be without incurring much culpability. By way of encouragement let it be noted, that greater success herein may be obtained than at first sight might seem possible. For myself, I could wish that the work of casting out from this storehouse that which is not worth keeping were a more easy matter than I find it. I am the owner of a huge mass of mental rubbish, which I frequently find to be worse than useless, inasmuch as it not only fills a space which might be better occupied, but also overlays much of what might be turned to good account. Often does some of this worthless, if not deleterious stuff turn up while I am searching for articles of a better description, and thus I am at once annoyed and hindered. My only consolation is, that it was not voluntarily admitted, but forced into its receptacle by means that I could neither prevent nor control. It would be idle to attempt to give the reader a catalogue of its multitudinous items. Suffice it to say, that, for their numbers and their heterogeneous character, they would bear a comparison with those which Milton has placed in the "limbo of vanity." I have long worked hard and earnestly in order to get rid of this mass, the best portion of which deserves no higher character than that of being harmless; while, as to the remainder, it could not be otherwise than baneful were it brought into activity. My success herein, although small, has yet been sufficient to warrant my making further efforts.

I commend these hints to any of my readers who may be similarly encumbered, believing that they will be found not wholly unworthy of their regard. If they be thereby prompted to make the like exertions, I doubt not of their success being quite sufficient to recompense their labour.

Secondly, if it be so difficult a matter to eject from the memory what is merely worthless, there should be especial care taken to guard against burdening it with even so much as

> "*One* fatal remembrance, one sorrow that throws
> Its bleak shade alike o'er our joys or our woes;"

for it is most true that only *one* wicked or even highly imprudent action may be the means of depositing in the storehouse of the mind such recollections as shall suffice to throw a deep and melancholy gloom over the whole remainder of life. Of this I formerly witnessed a saddening example in the case of a fellow-workman, who was, at that time, in many respects a worthy man, but he was unhappy. In his younger days he had quarrelled and fought with a companion, to whom he gave a fatal blow. He was held guiltless of murder, but the recollection of the sad incident embittered the cup of life through many a dreary year, until, in his old age, he was led to commit suicide. Who would not desire to be preserved from whatever might lead to such an issue? Who would not, with his whole heart, ejaculate,—" From all evil and mischief, good Lord, deliver us?" I make no further comment upon this admonitory anecdote, as it carries a moral with it, which of itself is sufficiently cautionary and instructive.

I now come, thirdly, to notice the evil of not usefully employing whatever of good may have been deposited in the memory; and I shall do this by giving an example in the form of a biographical sketch, as being more likely to interest the reader than if I were to adopt a merely didactic mode. The sketch will roughly delineate one (also a fellow-workman) whose memory was singularly retentive, and, moreover, abundantly stocked with useful matter, but which, as will be seen, he did not turn to any good purpose. I shall call him

THE LIVING DIRECTORY.

In several respects, besides that of his retentive power, this man was somewhat remarkable. In person he was tall, slender, and rather hungry-looking. He was at all times very meanly dressed, while his diet was of the plainest and cheapest kind. These privations, however, were the natural consequence of his very small earnings; for he was a slow and also an indolent workman. He was not, however, either ragged or dirty; while, in regard to diet, he professed to believe that quantity was of more importance than quality, and his seemingly thorough contentedness with coarse food warranted a belief that his profession was sincere. Yet, when better provision offered itself, he failed not to show that he could fully perform his part in helping to consume it. Thus, at a tailors' bean-feast, or a benefit-club dinner, or an election-treat, no one handled knife and fork with greater goodwill or with more effect. I will not venture to state how much in weight or measure he could quickly and comfortably dispose of, but it certainly was a very large quantity. As, however, these feasts were not of frequent occurrence, he usually had to fall back upon his tranquillising doctrine, that, if his stomach were but full, it did not much matter with what it was filled. And his practice fully accorded with his theory. I have often seen him attack an almost gigantic piece of bread with as much heartiness as if it had been food of the richest quality and of the most inviting flavour. With this, and perhaps a morsel of cheese, he would take a quart of cold water, and then seem to have made what he felt to be a good dinner. If the dinner hour came on, as sometimes it did, while he was walking in the fields, and he had no provender in his pockets, he generally found a substitute in a turnip, some blackberries or haws, or anything else that might be in season and within his reach.

The reader will have seen that this temperance in eating and drinking was but little praiseworthy, seeing that it was a matter not so much of choice as of necessity. Yet the example of contentedness with plain and even coarse diet is not unworthy of imitation, as, were it generally followed, there would be much less cause for the complainings of ill health and empty pockets that are now so frequent among working-people. He was successively a "loyal" volunteer and a local militiaman. His soldierlike appearance and his aptness at martial exercises seemed to indicate that soldiership was his proper vocation. But he was not a patriotic bearer of arms, being moved to take them up by considerations of a merely personal kind. A soldier's pay amounted to more than usually did his wages as a tailor, while the life of a soldier on home service gave more leisure than did his own profession. As to his courage I can say nothing, for he eschewed all such service as would have led him into the battle-field. My opinion, however, is, that upon the subject of fighting he held the doctrine which teaches that

> "He who fights, and runs away,
> May live to fight another day;
> While he who is in battle slain
> Can never rise to fight again."

Yet he might, had he been tried, have turned out to be fully as brave in spirit as he was soldier-like in aspect. However this may be, the life of a *marching* soldier would certainly have admirably suited his inquisitive spirit and observant habits; while his almost wonderful power of recollecting would have enabled him to give a full and an accurate detail of all that he might have witnessed. He seems, indeed, to have been from early childhood of the same or very similar habits, as will be apparent from the following statement.

When very young he was removed from his native town, and sent to London, where he was placed under the care of a relative who was engaged in the watchmaking business. Although more than forty years had passed over my workmate since he left London, he retained a lively recollection of the locality in which he had resided, and of numerous circumstances connected with it. He equally well remembered the many different branches into which watchmaking is divided, and could describe all the parts of a watch with great minuteness of detail. What has frequently moved my admiration was his clear recollection of the persons, dress, manners, and occupations of the people who lived near him; all which he would describe with as much readiness as if he had not been absent more than a few days. When he returned to his birth-place, he was apprenticed to a tailor who lived at a distance of about four miles from the town; and while thus situated he was sometimes sent thither by his master. On one of these occaions he is said to have met with an accident resembling that which befel the esquire of the renowned Don Quixote. Like his prototype, he was of a rather drowsy habit, and thus, while riding, would sometimes fall asleep. It seems that in this instance he slept so soundly as to lose his foot-hold upon the stirrups; when, as his nag was of low stature, while he was somewhat long-legged, his feet rested upon the ground. Although sleeping, he stood upright; and the then disburdened beast went on its way. Let the reader believe as much of this story as he may think to be credible. I vouch not for its entire truthfulness; but as I have often heard it told in his hearing without its eliciting from him any positive denial—and further, as I think he was quite likely to have fallen asleep at an unseasonable time, and in an unlikely place—I have here given it for the amusement of the reader.

As my hero was remarkable for his early and full knowledge of what was going on in his locality and its neighbourhood, he was jocularly called " The Mail," an appellation which he well deserved. His habit of rising very early had, doubtless, a good effect upon his mental as well as his physical constitution; and as he seldom failed to have a long walk in the fields before he went to work, he probably derived additional benefit * from this as well

* Herein, also, his example is worthy of imitation even by those who dwell in London or other large towns; for they likewise may enjoy a healthy morning walk, although they are not able to get into the green fields or the pleasant pathways of the country. The squares and principal streets of even the metropolis are in the early morning quiet enough for the purpose of walking, while the atmosphere is at that time comparatively pure and invigorating. If townspeople would but come back to the order of nature only so far as to retire early to rest, they would be very likely to learn the habit of early rising, a habit which has a far greater and more propitious influence upon health, whether intellectual, moral, or physical, than I will attempt to point out. Let any one duly make the experiment, and I have no fear concerning the result.

as from his practice of walking at all other convenient times. The state of the weather did not much affect him, so that, unless rain or snow were falling heavily, he went out as usual; nor did he seem to take any harm by being exposed to the rigours of either cold or heat.

Thus he had ample time for observation and inquiry; and by degrees he collected an amazing store of information upon various subjects. In regard to agriculture, I am inclined to believe that he knew much more about the soil, the capability, and the general state of the farms in the neighbourhood, than many of their owners or occupiers. His constant habit of closely observing the manner of carrying on farming operations, and of questioning the labourers about everything which he could not well understand, contributed greatly to his stock of knowledge. In like manner he gained much information concerning a good many handicraft trades and callings; so that, for aught that appeared to the contrary, he was well able to superintend, if not actually to work at them. To particularize them would be tedious; while from their number and variety I might seem to be exaggerating.

I think he had also some power of perceiving and enjoying the beauties of nature; for I have sometimes heard him speak of beautiful objects in a way that betokened genuine emotion. I especially recollect his having thus spoken on an occasion of witnessing the rising of the sun. Although it was at a rather unfavourable time—that of midwinter—yet even then the appearance of that glorious luminary, encircled as it was with masses of gorgeous and many-coloured clouds, was sufficient to call from him expressions that indicated feelings of mingled admiration and pleasure. Whether or not his thoughts ever ascended from nature to nature's God, I cannot determine. I regret that I must record of him the sad fact, that I never once heard him utter a word that betokened a belief in the existence of a Divine Being, or that manifested any concern about the state of man after he quits the body. From his boyhood upwards he had not (so far as I could learn) ever voluntarily united in public worship; yet he was a great frequenter of graveyards—as much so, perhaps, as was the venerable "Old Mortality" of the Waverley Novels. This, however, was merely for the purpose of amusement. He took great pleasure in perusing epitaphs, and in looking over the tombs and graves, by which means he refreshed his memory in regard to many whose bodies were there deposited, and of one or another of whom he would sometimes give an account. At length his own earthly course was ended, and he went into the invisible world.

In closing this account I cannot but express my regret that the subject of it seldom, if ever, aimed to be useful to his fellow-men. He was favoured with long life, and, as he possessed a considerable amount of practically useful knowledge, he might, had he so pleased, have been an instructor of many. Viewed as a steward in the service of the Great Master, he was greatly negligent, if not, indeed, unfaithful; and therefore must have gone hence very ill-prepared to give a good account of his stewardship. Here, however, I leave him; for I may not venture to judge concerning the issue of his final reckoning.

CHAPTER X.

In reverting to my personal history, I must again observe, that during the last few years the incidents connected therewith have been so few and commonplace as to be hardly worth the trouble of putting them into consecutive order;* yet, as it may not be amiss to pay some regard to dates, I may state that I have not, as yet, brought my story to the end of the year 1846. I have already said that I cannot well recollect recent events; and I here give proof of that avowal; for I cannot be sure as to the year in which occurred the first general failure of the potato-crop in Ireland. I think, however, that it was in this year. I do not, in general, find either leisure or inclination to think about public affairs; yet, as I am not wholly regardless of such as seem to be of more than ordinary interest or

---

* Notwithstanding what is said above, I am inclined to think that a record of sober thoughts and good feelings is likely to be more useful than a narrative of such incidents as occur in the everyday life of one situated like myself. If so, may I not conclude that a record of this kind, being a history of what is strictly personal, is within the proper boundaries of an autobiographical memoir? I regret that I have not been able to give an account of myself that would have approached nearer to my idea of such a memoir.

moment, the fearful calamity which had fallen upon the sister island could hardly fail of attracting my attention. In this instance, as in many others, I could not readily form a satisfactory opinion, because of the very conflicting accounts that were given in the public papers both as to the causes and the extent of the alleged failure; and I was equally perplexed in regard to the number of people whom that calamity had brought into a state of absolute want. It seemed, however, that there was no good ground for disbelieving that a heavy evil had come upon the Irish people. As to the evil itself, I had no difficulty in ascribing it to the permissive providence of Almighty God; but as to the causes of that evil, I felt, as I now feel, convinced that they must be ascribed to human agency. There had long been, as it seemed to me, a highly culpable neglect of due foresight and precaution on the part of the Irish of every class. Were I to point out the particular class which I deem to have been the most blameworthy, it would be that which for so long a time, and with such earnest protestations of sincerity, has professed to be especially devoted to the service of the nation. What proof is there that this professedly patriotic class ever made any suitable efforts to better the condition of the Irish people? Without fear of successful contradiction it may be affirmed that there is none. Even that eminent man who possessed so wonderful an influence over the popular mind, failed to use that influence in a right direction. With mental powers of no common order, and possessing ample means of employing those powers in a beneficial manner, he might have been the instrument of conferring a vast amount of genuine good upon those whom he was wont to call "the finest peasantry in the world." These people had such unbounded confidence in his wisdom and generosity as would have enabled him to carry out any patriotic or benevolent plan for improving their condition. What they really needed was, to be taught the value and necessity of industry, temperance, and prudent foresight, with every other habit that is conducive to personal comfort, domestic happiness, or social order; they would, doubtless, have as readily obeyed him in these truly useful matters, as they did in regard to political associations and movements. Had all the objects for which these agitations were carried on been obtained, they would probably have proved as utterly useless for any good purpose as the long coveted boon called "Catholic Emancipation." Instead of being taught to make a clamour for the restoration of a parliament, which, while it existed, was unquestionably one of the most corrupt and incompetent of legislative bodies, the peasantry of the sister island needed to be taught the necessity of cultivating something less liable to failure than the potato, and to aim at obtaining better food than the refuse portion of that equivocally useful root. Such matters as these, however, formed no part of the teaching which they received from their great leader or any of his coadjutors. Had they been duly instructed in these respects, it seems probable that the famine, with all its dreadful accompaniments and consequences, might have been prevented.

In the day of their country's calamity it does not appear that any special efforts to afford relief to the sufferers were made by the party I have named; on the contrary, they seem to have looked for the usual contributions to the Liberator's rent and the funds of the Repeal Association; while the vast amount of pecuniary aid given by the Parliament and people of England was regarded by them as a matter of right. The manner in which this benevolence was ultimately recompensed showed that the recipients had thoroughly learned the lessons of hatred to the Saxons which for so long a period had been given them by their Celtic teachers. Whether or not their chief was a true patriot, I will not presume to determine; if he were, I cannot but think that he greatly mistook his way, for the course which he pursued could not end in advancing his country's welfare. If, on the other hand, he were insincere in his professions of patriotism, then how deeply was he culpable in practising, as he so long did, upon the feelings of his ignorant and easily-excited countrymen, often leading them to the verge of rebellion by his intemperate orations, or the equally reprehensible manifestoes which he sent forth from Derrynane Abbey! It was mere trifling or trickery to caution the people against committing acts of violence while, at the same time, he more than insinuated the necessity of resorting to intimidation, in order to the obtainment of what he called "justice to Ireland."

In looking at his whole course by means of the best light which I can command, I am constrained to state that I cannot vindicate his conduct, except at the expense of his understanding. This, however, is what I dare not venture upon, and therefore shall leave the question to other and abler judges of both intellectual and moral character.

Passing from the consideration of his principles of action, I may, however, venture to give an opinion of his public conduct. In this I am well disposed to find matter for commendation, but I cannot readily do so; on the contrary, I am forced to believe that he did little or nothing that tended to promote the well-being of his countrymen, nor has left behind him any works of either piety or philanthropy that might testify of his virtues. It is very improbable that he will be much noticed by the future chroniclers of Irish history, for already he seems to be but little remembered even by his former admirers and disciples. But, be this as it may, I cannot believe that his name will go down to posterity with anything like the honour which will ever be attached to the names of such men as George Washington and Benjamin Franklin.

Whether or not his wretched countrymen will ever emerge from the almost fathomless depths of mingled demoralization and degradation in which they have long been immersed, is a problem which I will not attempt to solve. As, however, it was the work of many centuries—beginning long before they passed under English rule—to bring them into their present miserable condition, so most probably will it be the work of several successive ages to raise them from a state of worse than semi-barbarism to one of true civilization. When they shall have ceased to think about distinctions of race; when they shall no longer cherish the irritating feelings that spring from recollections of conquest on the one side, and of subjugation on the other; and when, moreover, they shall have learned practically to recognise that divine precept " Thou shalt love thy neighbour as thyself," then, but not till then, will they rise to the dignity and enjoy the immunities of a truly enlightened people; then, for the first time in its long-drawn history, will there be some propriety in calling Ireland

" —————————— Great, glorious, and free,
First flower of the earth and first gem of the sea!"

That such a time will come, I cannot doubt, although I fear that its advent is not at hand.*

Here, however, I must dismiss a subject which to me is not of an inviting character. It gives me no pleasure to dwell upon the faults and the follies of the Irish nation. So far as I have had any personal acquaintance or intercourse with Irishmen, I have nothing whereof to complain, but rather cause of commendation. I earnestly wish all peace and prosperity to Ireland, and thus take leave of the country and its people.

In what follows I shall probably again act the ungracious part of a censor; but, if I demean myself becomingly, perhaps I may stand excused for my seeming censoriousness.

The reckless speculations which were carried on in (I think) 1846 led me to reflect on the question of making haste to be rich. As I had in remembrance former times of a like kind, I was quite prepared for the adverse issue of the golden dreams in which such multitudes were now indulging. Nothing but an inordinate love of money could have so blinded many otherwise discerning people, as to have induced them to be purchasers of shares in the delusive (if not indeed fraudulent) railroad and

* I hardly need state that these remarks are not meant to apply to the whole population of the sister island, for I am glad to know that an exception must be made in regard to a large and, I hope, an increasing number.

I

other schemes of the day—schemes, many of which were so outrageously wild and visionary as to make it, at first sight, matter of surprise that any honest person of sound mind could be brought to support them. Yet even the wildest of these concerns found as much favour with the public as enabled its projectors to divide between them a considerable sum of money received in the shape of deposits.

The early abandonment of so many plausible schemes, and the small amount of deposit-money usually returned to the shareholders, seem to warrant the opinion that, in many instances, the only object of their projectors had been immediate personal gain; nor did the evil stop here, for, even in those cases where the proposed scheme was carried further, there was no small amount of iniquitous trickery practised in regard to the purchase or sale of shares. By the scandalous proceedings of mere gamblers, called speculators, the original price of shares was often greatly enhanced, although nothing could have been done which gave them an increased value. The loss sustained when they declined in price, which of necessity they soon did, was made to fall upon the honest and fair-dealing shareholder. That a vastly increased amount of bankruptcy and insolvency should be accumulated by these disgraceful speculations was to be expected; and, therefore, all observant people could easily account for the breaking-up of such a multitude of commercial and business men so soon after the speculating madness had begun to subside. As to the injury inflicted upon shareholders of private station and of small property by these gambling transactions, there can be no doubt that it was, in many cases, ruinous.

These calamitous issues to what had been said to promise great and permanent public advantage, contributed much to strengthen my long-standing and thorough dislike of all merely speculating traders. I cannot indeed help regarding them as belonging to the worst class of gamblers, and do most heartily wish that it were possible to put an effectual stop to their mischievous interference with legitimate and regular trading. Notwithstanding all that I may have read or heard in defence of speculators, I cannot but believe that all the good which they may have effected, if contrasted with the evil of which they have been the undoubted authors, would be but as a single drop of water in comparison with the "congregated wave" of the vast ocean, aided by

"Each river, cataract and lake."*

---

* This may, perhaps, be deemed an unfairly severe judgment, but may it not be easily borne out by reference to matters of fact, such, for example, as the interference of these men with the trade in cotton-wool? By means of their disreputable tricks they often bring about an advance in the price of this article sufficient to embarrass the master manufacturers, whilst it inflicts much misery on their multitudinous work-people. If it be true that they

As the following remarks refer to an incident which occurred in the year 1847, I shall now take leave of 1846. This incident was connected with a mode of doing business far more iniquitous than seems to be suspected. For myself, I have long regarded it as worse than highway robbery. It may be called "The Job System." If any of my readers is unaware of what is meant, the following story will explain it. I premise merely that the scene was the Court of Bankruptcy. A bankrupt under examination by his creditors' solicitor gave a fair account of his business transactions until the examiner came to an item which he could not clearly understand. On his questioning the bankrupt concerning it, the latter pleaded forgetfulness as an excuse for not giving the required information. He was then, naturally enough, requested to refer to his accounts, when he affirmed that he had kept none; but after some further delay he consented to recollect that he had sold the goods in question for about one-third of the price at which he had bought them of the manufacturer. This confession led to the purchaser of the goods being called, who very readily corroborated the bankrupt's statement, and was then dismissed with-

contrived to enhance the price of the food intended for the relief of the Irish people in the late famine, there is no need of any other examples either of their power or their willingness to be the agents of iniquity.

out one word being said to him, even by the Commissioner, as to the very reprehensible part which he had taken in the transaction. This omission of all reproof serves to show how generally practised is this fraudulent mode of doing business.*

I hardly need add anything to this story in order to explain what is meant when it is said that goods have been sold or bought as "a job." The goods are, of course, originally bought upon credit, and in all cases are sold for ready money. There is no doubt as to the fact that they are often bought for the express purpose of being thus disposed of. Fraudulent men buy them with a view to forward

---

* That it is generally well-known is evident from the fact that "job" goods are advertised for in the newspapers. I lately saw one of these advertisements in which it was announced that the advertiser would buy, for ready-money, "job goods of every kind, and to any amount." As a further inducement to the intending sellers of such bargains, it was added, that the buyer might be fully depended upon for observing the "strictest secrecy." The latter announcement will sufficiently show the moral quality of these transactions. From this advertisement it appears that even this species of trade is not without its due proportion of speculators, and it must be admitted that, in this case, the character of the trade seems to warrant the interference of these unscrupulous dealers. I may add that provision has been made for the convenience of "job" tradesmen by some considerate carmen, who inform the public that they are at all times ready to "remove goods of all kinds with secrecy and dispatch." By the way, I hold these to be among the disreputable advertisements which no newspaper proprietor ought to admit into his columns.

their selfish purposes; and it is to be feared that they are sometimes bought by needy men, who resort to this method of raising money wherewith to "stave off" for the present the evil day of settling with their creditors. In either case there is wrong doing, such as is both culpable and dangerous, tending, as it does, to the commission of crimes which jeopardize both body and soul.

A sad example of this was given some thirty years ago in the case of a reckless man, who first disposed of a large quantity of goods upon the "job" system, and then set fire to his warehouse, in order that he might be enabled to claim the full value of these goods from a Fire Insurance Company, upon the pretence that they had been burned. In this, however, he was frustrated, and soon afterwards was bankrupt. After this he "lived by his wits," as the phrase goes, until at length he outwitted himself. In an evil hour he took the chief part in the murder of a companion, for the sake of his money, and, being convicted of the crime, was brought to the gallows.

One word as to the systematic buyer of "job" goods. In the above case the buyer has done incalculable damage to upright, fair-dealing fellow-tradesmen, by vending his commodities at prices considerably below what would cover his outlay were the materials and workmanship duly paid for; and the injury hereby inflicted upon the workmen in his line of business is very great. Indeed, he must be "a bold, bad man" who dares to be its voluntary cause.

Neither is the public wholly guiltless in this matter. The prevalent and almost unexampled eagerness to buy at the cheapest possible rate, goes directly to the encouragement of this dishonest system of trading. Many worthy people now support it who probably would not were they aware of the base principles upon which it is carried on. There are, however, many who know all this, and yet give it their full countenance, attempting to justify themselves and the system by considerations of expediency or convenience. Are not these people partakers in other men's sins? I leave the reader to answer this question, while I go on to notice another social evil in which working men alone are implicated. I allude to that basely selfish method of getting a living which is most appropriately called " sweating,"* which very disreputable practice was invented about thirty-four years ago. At that time there was much distress among the journeymen tailors of London, in consequence of the cessation of war, which caused a great falling off in the supply of work, with a considerable increase in the number of workmen.† There was

* It may be as well to say that these remarks are intended to apply only to the workpeople of my own trade.

† The decrease in the amount of employment was chiefly in military and naval clothing, and the increased supply of labour was given by recently discharged soldiers and sailors.

barely employment for the clever hands, while many of those who were incompetent could get none. These combined circumstances, together with the embarrassed condition of some of the masters through the falling off in their business, afforded a convenient opportunity to selfish men to serve themselves. That this could only be done at the expense of others, of course gave them no uneasiness. They commenced operations by going about among the masters taking with them a well-made garment as a specimen of their workmanship, and offering to make up in a similar manner, and at one third less than the customary price, all the clothes which might be required. This offer was made to the worthy man by whom I was then employed, who declined accepting it; which however was not the case with a good many of the selfish or needy masters, and thus the "sweaters" obtained the means of carrying out their schemes.

They then hired incompetent workmen, among whom they distributed the work, after it had been "fitted up" or "marked" by themselves, and gave a general oversight as the work went on. By a judicious division of employment, they were enabled to get through a good deal of work in a comparatively short time. Thus the wages earned in a week, although on a reduced scale, were often in the aggregate as much as from four to five pounds; of which the "sweater," of course, came in for "the lion's share," his helpers being paid at a very low rate." It is easily to be seen that this method of working was highly profitable, and not a little pleasant to the "sweater," while it could not but be a sadly profitless and toilsome concern to his assistants. But the system admitted of being made yet more profitable; and therefore ere long the proper steps were taken to obtain this desirable issue. These consisted in becoming a purveyor of food for his men, and as both the quality and the price of this were regulated by himself, the speculation was not unsuccessful. Another addition was made to his income by the employment of women and children, as their help was to be had for a very trifling remuneration. Herein, however, it eventually turned out that the sweater had overshot his mark, for many of the women learned enough of the trade to qualify them for working without guidance. These set about trying to procure work at first hand, and, as they offered to take a lower price than was given to the middle-man, they had little difficulty in obtaining employment, at least by the dealers in ready-made clothes.

This was a heavy blow to the middle-man; but it was not the only one which fell upon him; for there soon arose a class of middle-*women*, whose helpers shortly became numerous enough to make up a large amount of work. This, of course, tended to lessen the supplies which the male "sweater" had been accustomed to obtain; and the diminished supply led in its turn to a reduction in his former charges, to enable him to regain his lost ground. Then arose a competition between the male and female "sweaters," which eventually did great injury to both parties, while it brought their hapless and helpless assistants into a state of the most miserable poverty and degradation. All this might have been avoided, had those who introduced the "sweating" system been as good men as they were clever tailors. They were under no necessity to adopt unworthy expedients, as there were at hand the means of obtaining such relief as would have kept them from pressing want. The trade clubs were then in existence, and were well supported by the principal master-tailors; so that really good workmen (if at all of decent character or appearance) were seldom without as much work as would have sufficed to procure them a maintenance. There was also a fund maintained by each club, for the purpose of assisting unemployed workmen; the allowance from which was at the rate of two days' wages per week, the wages at that time being six shillings per day. This fund was well supported by the employed workmen; for, although it was sometimes necessary to levy a large contribution, in order to provide the required sum, I do not recollect that it ever failed to answer its purpose.* The relief given was, as I believe, suffi-

* I remember to have paid as much as five shillings for one week's contribution; but I paid it cheerfully, as also, I

cient to have kept the recipients from distressing privation; and, if so, it is evident that the men who invented the "sweating" system, were moved thereto by selfishness rather than necessity.

During the last forty-five years, I have seen much that has tended to make me believe, that the worst enemies of working-people belong to their own class. Were I asked why I believe this, I should answer first, Because working-people are necessarily far better acquainted, than any of the higher classes can be, with the vulnerable points in the circumstances of their compeers; and, therefore, when about to invade their rights, or to give them pain, they can make the attack with greater skill, and, consequently, with a greater probability of success, than persons of higher station and different habits would be able to do. Secondly, I should say, that although many members of the upper classes may be willing enough to become oppressors, they are restrained from fully carrying out their evil wishes by considerations of self-respect or some other personal motive; whereas among uneducated people it is seldom that this restraining influence is felt. They do not in general seem to take any heed as to what is due to their own character, their only considerations being such as relate to mere expediency or convenience. If

believe, did nearly all the contributors. The existence of such a resource served to give a feeling of confidence to every member of the club.

their object be attainable without much risk of personal danger, they readily employ whatever means they can command for effecting it; I have witnessed many instances of this, which, although I was not the sufferer, have deeply grieved me. Were I to notice the subject of trading, I should be forced to give a similar opinion as to the readiness manifested by poor people to injure their fellows; for, among petty dealers of every description, there are many who are guilty of fraudulent conduct, and thus inflict much injury upon their customers, who are principally working people. This selfish spirit is also often to be seen among men who work in the same shop; and of this I will give an example, premising that, as I was not injured thereby, I am the less likely to be guilty of exaggeration. The most striking display of selfishness which I ever witnessed, was in the conduct of one whom I shall call

THE SELFISH WORKMAN.

He was healthy and active, temperate, frugal, and diligent; a good and very quick workman. He was married, but had no children; in addition to all these advantages, he was strong-minded and very well-informed upon all common matters. Thus he could plead neither necessity nor ignorance in justification of his very disreputable conduct. It is the custom of journeymen tailors while at work, to perform for each other sundry little services, which, while they are helpful to the one party, are in no way burdensome to the other. They were, however, grudged by my shopmate; yet, as he feared reprisals if he altogether refused, he contrived to avoid being again troubled on this score, by performing them in such a manner as to give much additional annoyance instead of assistance. All this he would do with such seeming good will, as made it difficult to believe that he had intentionally done wrong. If, however, he was suspected of this, it was quite useless either to remonstrate or to be angry, for he was not to be moved by such means; on the contrary, he was quite as merry about it as if it had been nothing more than a harmless and allowable joke. As he was able to manifest at all times what seemed to be a thoroughly good temper, and, moreover, had at command some ready wit and humour, he not only got easily out of the scrape, but also continued to retain some hold upon the good will of his fellow-workmen. To tell the truth, he was so adroit in the management of such matters, that it would have been next to impossible to be seriously angry with him. When called to work in partnership with another man, he seldom failed to have the best of the bargain; for, as he was a skilful and quick workman, he was pretty sure to be ahead of his partner; and thus could select for his own use all the best parts of the materials; while, as he was the first to get through the job, he could as easily contrive to leave sundry little things undone, which, of course, had to be done by his less active helpmate. He was wont to keep up his strength, while at work, by means of a liberal, but not excessive allowance of porter; concerning the inventor of which, he often affirmed that he "deserved to sleep in the Elysian fields." Thus much for his shopboard exploits; I must now give a brief account of his doings as an acquaintance and a man of business. As to the first of these characters the following story will suffice, to show how he could enact it. Some of his fellow workmen having proposed to visit him, at the usual time for tailors' visits, namely, on a Sunday morning; he, with much seeming heartiness, sanctioned their proposal, promising to give them a cordial reception. On going to his house, however, they found out their mistake; for, instead, of admitting them, he presented himself at one of the first-floor windows, and informed them that he was not at home. To have expected admission after this announcement would have been quite idle; so they measured back their steps, and were obliged to be as contented as possible after such provoking treatment. Whenever this trick was referred to, he was greatly amused, and failed not to have another hearty laugh at the expense of his visitors. In his character of a business man, I cannot present him under an aspect even so favourable as the foregoing. What I have heard I will repeat, just as it was related in his presence, and as he admitted that he had done what he was charged with, and, moreover, made sport of it, I have no doubt of its entire truthfulness. In one instance he sold to an unsuspecting buyer twelve gaiters, which, of course, the purchaser understood to form six pair of those useful articles. They were however adapted for one leg only, and thus there were twelve more required, in order to make the others of service. As he was a total stranger to the buyer, he came off scatheless; and not only pocketed his ill-gotten pelf, but also made himself very merry about the trick. In another case he disposed of the lease and good-will of a house; in which by the aid of his wife he had been carrying on the business of a chandler; but as the purchaser omitted to guard against being over-reached, my workmate (as would have been expected by any one who knew him) took advantage of that omission, by taking another house in the same neighbourhood, and drawing thither as many of his former customers as he could persuade to deal with him. At the recital of even this trick, wicked as it was, he always seemed much amused.

After having perused these statements, the reader will be prepared for my telling him, that my workfellow, in regard to religious belief, was a *nothingist*. He would have had it believed that he was a deist; but as this title, when applied to unlearned men, means a practical atheist, I prefer describing him by such a word as I have ventured to use.

As I wished to ascertain whether or not he had any moral consciousness, I observed him somewhat closely; but, with all my care, I could never discover that he had any. I do not say that his conscience had become seared or dead, for I believe that he never had one. The germ of the moral sense, in his case, seemed never to have been brought from its embryo state. Thus he naturally became a being superior to a mere animal only in regard to his intellectual faculty, which in him was truly a poor pre-eminence, as it served no better purpose than that of enabling him the more cleverly to do evil.

In putting the finishing touch to this somewhat dark picture, I may observe, that although it is more than thirty years since I saw its original—who even then had passed the meridian of life—I think it probable that he is yet on this earth. If so, most sincerely do I wish that long ere now he may have profitably read the Scriptures (of which, without knowing their contents, he was wont to speak most contemptuously), and have learned to honour Him of whom they testify so far as no longer to call him by names to which I may not give utterance.

I could easily present other pictures of a similarly unpleasing character; but this alone will, if duly studied, be sufficient to teach more than one deeply interesting and admonitory lesson, while I shall be at liberty to notice other subjects.

CHAPTER XI.

At the time about which I am now writing the public journals were much engaged with certain subjects, of which the first that I shall glance at relates to the duty of acting consistently in the conduct of public affairs. Although readily admitting the obligatory nature of this duty upon statesmen, yet I was unable to join in the severe censures that were then cast upon an eminent man on account of his alleged inconsistency. These rebukes seemed to be much more severe than the conduct complained of would justify, even were it fully as culpable as it was affirmed to be. Moreover, I doubted the propriety of calling the alleged offence by the name which had been given to it; for if a change in the opinions and consequent policy of a statesman is culpable, however much such a change may be called for by altered circumstances, it seems to follow that all other persons are bound to avoid altering their opinions, and of course their conduct, however foolish or vicious that conduct may be. To what direful mischief all this would necessarily lead, were it rigorously carried out, I hardly need say, as any one may see that it would tend both to the perpetuation of every existing evil, and the prevention of all attempts to carry on the work of improvement. But I am not sure that the offence alleged was the real cause of all this angry feeling towards the presumed offender. On the contrary, I suspect that its true source might be found in the presumed tendency of the conduct complained of to break up and disperse a large, compact, and hitherto very influential political party—a party having sufficient power to check, and sometimes to control, the Government. If, however, this were admitted to have been the ground of offence, I should still be unable to join in rebuking the great and good man referred to; for after all that I have read and heard about political parties, I am wholly unable to see either their utility or their expediency. What is wanted—and which I should much rejoice to see—is the total subversion of all parties, and the substitution in their stead of an assembly consisting of good and able men, among whom the only rivalry would be that right noble one of endeavouring to be the most extensively useful.

I glance, secondly, at the war question, upon which there was much said which to me seemed to be mere declamation, with a good deal of positive assertion, unsupported by any adequate evidence. After all that was affirmed the question seemed to be just as much unsettled as before, nor do I think that it will or can be satisfactorily decided unless there were at hand more direct and authoritative testimony than is now obtainable. It were better, therefore, to avoid coming to conclusions, which, however just they may seem to be, must be drawn from inadequate or doubtful premises. If reference be made solely to what is matter of undoubted fact, there will not be much, if indeed any difficulty in perceiving that the evidence in favour of the views taken by the one party is pretty nearly balanced by that which justifies those of the other. There is consequently much cause for doubting as to the side upon which the weight of this evidence really preponderates, and therefore it is hard to say which side has the best of the argument. If, for example, the worthy people who affirm that war, under all possible circumstances, is unjust and indefensible, be asked for the authority upon which they make this affirmation, they must confess that there is no declaration, either preceptive or otherwise, in the Sacred Scriptures, to that effect; and it is plain that if this authority fails them they can have no other. On the other hand, those who maintain that war, especially that which is strictly defensive, has some claim to be deemed justifiable, have a considerable amount of presumptive or indirect evidence in favour of their opinion. The testimony of all history, both sacred and secular, shows that war in itself is a terrible evil. It equally shows that it is not necessarily an unalleviated evil. Nay, it goes further; for it proves, beyond all successful contradiction, that this justly reprobated practice has been made the pioneer of true civilization, where previously all was wretched and degrading barbarism. If this great fact be duly considered, it will perhaps seem best to let the abstract question rest, and, in the mean while, to do all that can possibly be done towards either removing or preventing the causes of war. Thus the very praiseworthy advocates of universal good will among men will be preparing the way for the advent of the Prince of Peace, under whose righteous and benignant government

> "All crimes shall cease, and ancient fraud shall fail,
> Returning Justice lift aloft her scale,
> Peace o'er the world her olive-branch extend,
> And white-rob'd Innocence from heaven descend."

Then, but not till then, shall men "beat their swords into ploughshares and their spears into pruning-hooks; nation shall not lift up sword against nation, neither shall they learn war any more." Let, then, the advocates of universal peace take encouragement, and continue to discourage everything which tends to foster those fruitful causes of all quarrels — the bad passions of the human heart. They may not be successful to the extent of their wishes, but assuredly they will not labour in vain, although it may not be given them to see the issue of their benevolent efforts. When these hitherto dominant passions shall have been fully and finally subdued, then shall "wars cease unto the ends of the earth," and there shall be " an abundance of peace so long as the moon endureth."

I now come to the third of these controverted questions: that of " Capital Punishments." Concerning the discussions upon this subject I have to make the same remarks as in the preceding case: the question cannot be definitely settled, because the only book from which authoritative evidence could be drawn affords no decisive testimony; the controversy, therefore, had better be terminated. In dismissing it, I take occasion to remark that, about fifteen years ago, I heard it discussed by two able men, each of whom was well read in biblical learning. At the close of that discussion I perceived that the disputants had left the matter just where they found it, and ever since then I have felt convinced that the question must be left open; and further, that all reasonings about it ought to be governed by considerations either of state policy or public feeling. For myself, I am decidedly favourable to the discontinuance of capital punishments, although I am of opinion that they are not unsanctioned by Divine revelation; while they are (as I think) supported by the general usages both of civilized and barbarous nations. I therefore say, upon this as upon many other knotty questions, " Let every man be fully persuaded in his own mind," and leave others to judge for themselves.

Were I to consider another of these subjects, viz. that of " Sabbath Observance," I should be obliged to make observations very similar to the foregoing. While I have no doubt as to the high value of the Sunday, whether considered as a day of rest or of devotion, I am unable to affirm that there is any positive and distinct scriptural testimony as to the precise manner of observing it; all the evidence relates to the far more important question of the spirit in which it ought to be observed. In stating this, however, I am anxious not to be misapprehended, for I have long been thoroughly persuaded that it is an imperative duty to recognise and honour the sabbath by a regular and devout attendance upon public worship, no less than by a conscientious attention to private and family devotion.

I have but a slender account to give of my reading during the year 1847; yet I had the pleasure of perusing Bishop Horne's very beautiful Commentary on the Book of Psalms. An introductory Essay, written by that justly eminent man Mr. James Montgomery, was prefixed, and gave to the work much additional attraction. I also read two volumes written by that worthy, but very unhappy gentleman, the Rev. Blanco White. One of these was made up of letters which originally appeared in the 'New Monthly Magazine,' under the signature of Don Leucadio Doblado. This I had previously read, but was well pleased at being enabled to give it a second perusal. The other volume, whose title, however, I cannot recollect, contained a very impressive account of the Spanish church and clergy. Were it seemly in one like myself to do so, I should strongly recommend each of these works to the especial attention of those young clergymen of our own established Church who may be in danger of becoming as deeply unhappy as was, and (if living) probably still is, the author of the 'Nemesis of Faith.' Such works as these might serve as beacons to warn them of the rocks or quicksands towards which they may be drifting, at the imminent hazard of being wrecked.

Here I dismiss the year 1847, and proceed to notice its successor—a year which will ever be remarkable for its having given birth to events of no ordinary importance—events of much flattering promise, which, however, was soon followed by bitter disappointment. Although I had not for many years thought much about political matters, I was now almost constrained to notice them. As the current of the popular mind, both on the Continent and at home, seemed to run towards the republican form of government, I was naturally led to consider the comparative merits of republics and monarchies. There is something about the former which is so pleasing to the fancy of unreflecting people, that I do not wonder at its finding such general favour. For instance, there is the idea of equality in rank, together with notions about a more equal distribution of property, a larger amount of political influence, and an increase of social immunities. All this is very inviting, especially when viewed, as it commonly is, through the deceptive medium of a heated and unchecked imagination. Yet, after all, there is good reason for doubting whether the republican form of government be much if at all superior to the monarchical. If the testimony of history be worthy of credit, it seems to warrant the opinion that it is not. Neither in the Grecian, Roman, or Italian republics did the common people possess greater means of domestic or personal comfort than they might have obtained under a monarchy. Even the English Commonwealth, though superintended by a man of extraordinary ability, was a failure. It is quite plain that it had not bettered the condition of the people, or they would not so generally and quietly have acquiesced in its subversion. A second experiment would probably be not more successful; and therefore it behoves all who assume to be either the political instructors of the public mind, or the advocates of popular rights, to be very careful lest they should become the instruments of damaging, rather than of improving, the public interests. Legislators and journalists may decry a monarchy, and laud a commonwealth, in language which to them may seem of harmless tendency, but which, however, may sink deeply in many hearts, be talked about in workshops and factories, beer-houses and gin-palaces, and then brooded over in habitations made wretched by *other* causes than popular wrongs, until it becomes the parent of conspiracy or rebellion. The necessity for this carefulness is made all the greater, because working-men seldom read on more than one side of any political question, while that side is pretty sure to be the one that is most likely to excite strong prejudices against royalty and all other monarchical institutions or usages.

When it is remembered that many of the cleverest of these politicians are recklessly imprudent or intemperate, and consequently miserably poor, and moreover that they, almost without exception, ascribe their poverty to any cause but the true one, it will be seen how highly imprudent, if not dangerous, it is to furnish them with a pretext for attributing it either to a wrong form of government, or to the mal-administration of public affairs. That a large amount of popular discontent, having a perilous tendency, may be, and often is, produced both by speeches in Parliament and by leading-articles in newspapers, I am fully convinced; and it may be well to add, that my conviction arises not from hearsay, but from careful and long-continued observation. I respectfully submit these plain remarks to the consideration of those whom they concern, and gladly dismiss a subject which to me has long ceased to be attractive.

The preceding observations lead me, by a natural train of thought, to those which follow. I have usually found that my compeers who professed and who were believed to be learned in political theories were greatly deficient in the art of self-government, and also, if family-men, in that of ruling their households. Yet how can he who is overtasked by the work of governing himself or his family expect to be equal to the government of many millions? This, however, is a reflection which, although so obvious, they seem never to have made. On the contrary, they appear to think themselves very superior men to those who, disregarding politics, give their undivided attention to their proper duties. I have often heard these praiseworthy men taunted on account of their political ignorance, and told that this ignorance was the cause of their contentedness. To me, however, it was evident that they could give a far better reason for it, as they were decently clothed, sufficiently fed, and not badly lodged. These little matters, be it observed, go a great way towards making a man quiet and contented. They had moreover the satisfaction of knowing that all these comforts were, under Providence, the fruits of their own industry and prudence, and this knowledge served to make them yet more satisfied. On the other hand, I knew a man who had neither wife nor children to provide for, who was blessed with good health, and was clever at his business, yet was ragged, ill-fed, and badly housed. This man was a tap-room oracle and orator, whom his pot-companions believed to be deeply read in all political matters. He was, however, a drunkard, negligent of his work, and consequently miserably poor. That he was discontented with the government followed as a matter of course; for in these, as in other cases of folly or vice, there is a great unwillingness to ascribe the evils endured to their true causes. I have known other men of like character and habits who have adopted the same means of endeavouring to avoid self-accusation, making a scapegoat of the government; while all around them could plainly see that their wretched state was the necessary consequence of their own folly. Such men as these are powerless for any good purpose, but they are very far from being so in regard to evil, being, as might be expected, the warm advocates of Socialism, Chartism, or any other wild scheme which promises to bring them a good living at little cost; and as they manage to obtain a considerable share of notice, they damage the characters of their worthier fellow-workmen, of whom they are believed to be true specimens. They are sometimes the means of obstructing the great work of popular improvement, as, for example, by making themselves conspicuous in acts of a riotous or otherwise disorderly character.

My purpose in making these remarks is to do what I can towards guarding the well-disposed portion of the working classes against whatever might tend to identify them with disreputable or dangerous men. It were easy to show the necessity for their being cautious, by considerations of a prudential character; but, as example is more striking, and in general more pleasing, than precept, I prefer taking that course, and will cite one, which, although it has been published, and I would hope extensively read, is yet sufficiently impressive and interesting to warrant my introducing it here. I shall give it, as nearly as I can, in the language of my informant, and in a distinct form, calling it

SOME ACCOUNT OF SAMUEL BAMFORD.

All that I know of this worthy man was derived from the letters of an intelligent and judicious friend, who in the year 1845 gave me the following account:—" The author of the work to which I referred in a former letter is Samuel Bamford, a silk-weaver. He took part in that celebrated meeting of Reformers which was held at Petersfield near Manchester, when that melancholy destruction of human life took place which was so emphatically designated by Sir Francis Burdett as 'the Manchester massacre.' In my humble opinion the author of 'Passages in the Life of a Radical' was the wisest and best man of the many thousands which composed the assembly referred to; yet he was marked out for prosecution, on the charge of having disturbed the public peace. He was tried, found guilty, and sentenced to be imprisoned in Lincoln Castle. If you have not read his work you will perhaps be reminded, by these statements, both of the man and his misadventures. I observe, concerning his narrative, that it is marked by a clearness and simplicity of style which I hold that none but an author of superior powers is able to adopt. There does not appear to be even so much as one redundant word, nor does there seem to be one word wanting. That his mental qualifications are of a high order I infer from the absence of all pretensions to learning; while, nevertheless, I think it probable that some who belong to what is denominated 'the educated class' would cut a sorry figure if compared with this untaught, but very able man. That he is a *good* man, as well as a man of knowledge and ability, I conclude from the strong and pleasing evidence which the work affords of his true conjugal love, as that species of love cannot be felt by a *bad* man. When he mentions his wife his true character shines through his words, although, probably, he was quite unconscious of the fact.

" I here remark that, after all the complaints that are so frequently made about the rareness of humane or generous feelings, Samuel Bamford found that the Lincolnshire magistrates were both kind-hearted and candid men—well disposed to make their prisoner as comfortable as was consistent with his being kept in safe custody. He became ill, and, as he required a nurse, he expressed to the magistrates his wish that his wife should be allowed to nurse him. These very worthy gentlemen readily gave their permission. She came, and, after her services as a nurse were no longer needful, was, to the honour of the magistrates, permitted to remain with him, upon the very easy condition that this indulgence should not then be made public. In the conduct of his wife we see the strength and the tenderness of woman's love in striking and most delightful combination. How readily was personal liberty sacrificed to the claims of conjugal affection! To be a prisoner was not felt to be a hardship, so long as thereby a husband's comfort might be provided for and secured. I regard the conduct of the wife as having been truly noble. At the close of the husband's imprisonment he took leave of the kind and indulgent magistrates in a manner that would have been creditable to any man, and then, with his excellent partner, went on his homeward journey. They were poor and almost destitute; yet they cheerfully pursued their wearying way, in hope of again seeing their only child, that child being a daughter. I do not remember the sequel, and therefore must here end my account of this good man. As to his book, I am of opinion that it is worthy of being kept in circulation on account of its delineating a beautiful moral picture, while I further believe that it deserves to be considered as an authority in regard to an important public event."

Believing that this brief account of Samuel Bamford is adapted to answer the end of its being given, I now bid him farewell—wishing him and his worthy partner, if they be yet in this life, all possible happiness.

Here I had thought to have escaped from the entangled and entangling meshwork of public matters; but I must not omit to remark on the danger of allowing large assemblages of the populace. To this I am moved by what I have been compelled to witness, no less than by what I may have read or heard. On the day when the Chartist leader called together his pupils and admirers upon Kennington Common, for the ostensible purpose of petitioning, but, as I believe, for that of intimidating Parliament, they were, through the admirable preventive means employed, kept from breaking the public peace; yet that meeting was made the occasion of no trifling disorder in the neighbourhood. Not far from my residence there assembled a miniature mob, consisting chiefly of the fearfully depraved youths with whom the locality abounds, who, headed by a few of more mature age, forthwith made a riotous movement, in the course of which they plundered many shops, and threw the whole district into a state of no little alarm and confusion. As the police force of the place had been greatly reduced by reason of the men having been called to do duty at Kennington, there were no efficient means of speedily putting a stop to the riot; and for several hours it went on, threatening very serious consequences. At length the alarm was quieted by the arrival of an auxiliary body of police, and in a short time order was restored; the damage done was, however, very considerable, and in some instances ruinous. This outbreak, with its consequences, served to confirm me in my opinion respecting the tremendous evils necessarily resulting from mob-ascendancy. This ascendancy ought, as I have long believed, to be prevented, at whatever cost. It is no less merciful to the intending rioters, than it is just towards well-disposed and quiet people, to employ, without delay and in the fullest degree, the most coercive means, in order to prevent or disperse all large gatherings of the populace, when congregated for political purposes. A moderate amount of wholesome severity at the outset would prevent the necessity for exercising much more at a subsequent stage of the proceedings. These remarks, however, are not meant to apply to popular meetings when consisting entirely of the people residing in or about the places where they are held; yet even such meetings as these are not quite unobjectionable, unless they be sanctioned by those who are charged with the preservation of the public peace.

CHAPTER XII.

HERE I turn from subjects which, but for the desire of being useful to others, I should not have even glanced at. My chosen pathway goes in a far different direction than that of politics, and I return to it, nothing doubting that I shall find something therein which may be applied to a good purpose. At my very entrance thereon I realize my expectation; for I come upon what forcibly reminds me of one from whom, while he was in this life, I received much courteous treatment, and of whom I now entertain a grateful remembrance. He went a few years ago to a foreign land, in quest of health; there he died, and, as he was a Protestant, his remains were deposited in unconsecrated ground; but whether or not a monumental stone marks their resting-place, I cannot tell. As he had been an able man and a good scholar, he might, as I think, have raised for himself a literary monument, such as would have proved more durable than one of marble. This, however, he omitted to do, and therefore is likely to be ere long wholly forgotten. But such record of him as I can give he must not want, for I shall never be forgetful of his good-will and kindly help. That he was not free from the defects common to human nature is more than probable; but with these I have nothing to do; and if I had I should be disposed to conceal rather than to expose them, for it pleases me much more to contemplate his virtues than to dwell upon his faults. That he was a lover of genuine truth and goodness I cannot doubt. What I saw of his conduct in relation to an aged and necessitous parent gave good proof that his affections were healthy and vigorous; and I could not but feel greatly-increased respect for him on this account. Hoping again to see him when I also shall have " put on immortality," I now "part company," and pursue my onward course. In doing this I am soon in view of that which tells me of another whom I shall not again look upon while I remain here. This was one of the companions of my childhood, and, moreover, my first instructor in the elements of writing and arithmetic. In after life we usually lived far apart, meeting only at long intervals. For many years, however, this separation was greatly compensated by a regular epistolary correspondence; of his share in which I might fairly speak in terms of warm commendation, for it was marked by good sense and right feeling, while it contained much interesting information concerning foreign lands, and the spirit-stirring scenes of military life. *He* also died far away from his native country, in a colony of the British Empire; and there his mortal part is now being resolved into its original elements. I think of him often, and never without a pensive feeling, which, if my thoughts in times of sadness did not "lie too deep for tears," might perhaps sometimes issue in an outward expression of sorrow. Yet I do not think of him with unalleviated regret. Many years ago he expressed in a letter his benevolent desire that when I should depart hence it might be my privilege to be permitted to "enter in through the gates into the city" of the blessed, and I now reciprocate his kindly feeling, by expressing my earnest hope, that he may, since he went hence, have been a citizen of the

"—————— Jerusalem above,
　The seat of everlasting love."

If such is *his* high privilege, and *I* should be wise enough to walk to the end of the path leading thereto, we shall again meet and resume an intercourse which shall no more be interrupted. These are reflections which, although to the gay and the thoughtless they may appear saddening, are nevertheless quite compatible with feelings of genuine cheerfulness. This I can testify from much and long-continued experience, so that I am fully convinced, that there is a close connection between the

"True taste of life, and constant thought of death."

Indeed, when one is cut off from nearly all intercourse with the living, as I have long been, the thoughts naturally turn to those who have gone hence. In common speech they are called the dead, but they are not dead, they are living, active, and intelligent spirits. Such of them as I knew and loved, while they were here, I continue to love with unabated sincerity and tenderness. With these I hold converse, which, although it be imaginary, is sometimes such as to touch the heart with almost the force of reality. Let not these reveries be deemed of little worth, for by their aid many an hour of constrained retirement or seclusion may be kept from becoming a time of dreary and depressing solitude. There may be in reserve, for even the most sociable and lighthearted, many a wearying season, during which they must either find solace in their own thoughts, or be left nearly if not quite destitute of consolation. The gay and the frivolous are not likely to become the voluntary visitors of the sick or infirm, even though the sufferers may in former days have been among their choice companions. They who regard the visitation of these sufferers as a part of their duty, and, moreover, endeavour to perform that duty, are not able to pay either frequent or lengthy visits to individuals, while the necessary duties of a household will in general still more curtail them. These or similar privations may fall to the lot of any one among those who are now blessed with health and activity; and they would therefore do well to aim at being prepared to endure them in a patient and resigned spirit.

As these observations were not premeditated, so neither have been the following; and on this account I deem them the more worthy of special regard. It is, indeed, possible that they were suggested by what preceded them; but as this seems doubtful, I am disposed to believe that they proceeded from another and a higher agency. It is not, however, needful that I should dwell upon this subject; and therefore I come, without further preface, to address those who may be, in their own persons, a good deal conversant with bodily illness or infirmity. Here, again, I shall prefer an example which is taken from facts, and which I recommend to the best attention of the reader, calling it

THE INVALID.

The subject of this sketch was one who, in early life, was called to exchange health and vigour for incurable disease. His sufferings continued during the course of nearly five successive years, during which they were sometimes very severe; while, in the intervals of comparative ease, he was borne down by great debility. Thus he needed continuous and tender nursing; and, so far as was possible, he had it, but there were times when he could not be duly attended to. He, however, made no complaint, but cheerfully endeavoured to do all he could towards helping himself; yet he was grateful for even the smallest amount of aid which at any time he received from others. His conversation and demeanour were always indicative of a patient and cheerful spirit. He was careful not to be troublesome, and equally anxious to help others. Although so young, he had learned to recognise the hand of Divine Providence in regard to his affliction, and expressed his entire willingness to bear whatever amount of pain or feebleness might fall to his lot. Thus he went on, until it became evident to those about him that he was nearly at the end of his earthly course; of which he also was himself conscious: but it gave him no uneasiness. When called to look death in the face, he did so steadfastly and calmly. His remaining power of utterance was spent in expressions of gratitude to those who had cared for him, of earnest wishes for their welfare, and of a " sure and certain hope" of the future blessedness both of himself and them. To these expressions he added that emphatical prayer, " Thou Son of David, have mercy upon me." These were his last words. After the lapse of a few hours from this time, he left the body, but in so quiet a manner that the precise moment of his departure was imperceptible.

Here the reader will please to consider me as having entered upon the year 1849; a year also pregnant with events of no common order, which, if duly considered, might even now be made subservient to the highly important purposes both of instruction and admonition. The chief of these events was the breaking out and subsequent ravages of that virulent disease, cholera; during the prevalence of which I saw much proof that those who are not thankful for national blessings are not likely to be humbled by national calamities. Yet I was much cheered when I observed the very becoming manner in which our rulers, together with multitudes of the people, avowed their belief in the doctrine of a divine and overruling Providence. A nation, in like manner as an individual, which " observes a Providence, will never want a Providence to observe." This recognition of God's authority over the nations, and of his superintendence of human affairs, is, I hope, far more general among our statesmen and legislators than it formerly was, and augurs well for the continuance of our national peace and the increase of our national prosperity.

Although I have expressed my dislike to political disquisitions, yet sometimes I can hardly avoid what seems to look in that direction. In what follows this may perhaps appear to be the case; but it will be only in appearance. The course of public business in Parliament suggested the thoughts which

I am about to set down—relating to the question of reform, but not of that kind to which the attention of our legislators was directed. I meddle not with that, as it would not only be an unpleasing topic, but also would be beside my purpose. My concern is with a species of reformation which is of paramount importance; as, without this, all other reforms are of little value. This is self-reformation, an improvement in morals and habits, of which there is obviously the most pressing need on the part of multitudes who are clamorous for an extension of their political privileges, or an amendment of their social condition. To this most important matter, however, these people are either quite indifferent or avowedly hostile; but could they be brought to think soberly about it, they would probably soon perceive, that, without a general moral reformation, there can be no adequate security for the continuance of any improvement which might be made in their political or social state. As to the further carrying out this improvement, it is what could hardly be looked for by any; for, until men in general are governed by good principles, there will always be enough of evil agency at work to endanger the public interests. It were well if this fact were more commonly recognised by all who feel interested about the work of either political or social improvement, and I venture to commend it to the earnest and abiding attention of the candid reader.

Another of the public topics to which I was induced to give some attention was that of taxation; the discussions upon which subject led me to a consideration of several taxes which press upon many with an almost ruinous weight, but which are nevertheless both self-imposed and cheerfully paid. These taxes, of course, are of the indirect kind, and therefore the less perceptible. Yet this is precisely the kind of taxation which, in the public imposts, gives rise to innumerable complainings; and it is worthy of remark that very many of those who are clamorous for a retrenchment in the national expenditure, with a view to a reduction of taxation, are voluntarily among the principal supporters of that expenditure, and consequently of the taxes, by being large consumers of several heavily-taxed articles, which, be it remembered, are not necessary either for health or nourishment, but are mere luxuries, and in many cases not a little pernicious. The reader will probably be prepared for my telling him that I here refer to " fire-water " and tobacco.

This example of self-taxation is a striking one, and might perhaps be sufficient for my purpose. I will, however, cite one or two more. First, there is the habit, so common among working men, of spending one or two days of each week in a worse than useless manner. During these days there is often a far heavier drain made upon their resources than by what they pay of public taxes during a much longer time. Then there is the habit of eating to excess, and this is frequently made the more chargeable by the use of articles which (as the phrase goes) are " in season." Thus, I have seen my fellow-workmen pay upwards of two shillings for a dinner neither more wholesome nor more plentiful than my own, for which I paid but sixpence. I have also seen them pay eightpence or upwards for the breakfast, including the morning dram, when a better meal could have been bought for fourpence.

Another self-imposed tax is that which is paid by means of the tippling and gambling which, in too many cases, form the amusements of the evening. I might give other examples, but I forbear, as these will suffice to show that no perceptible benefit would accrue to these self-taxed people by the repeal or reduction of the public imposts. If the leaders of the popular mind will use their influence towards relieving the people from this voluntary taxation, they will thereby be likely to serve them far better than they have hitherto done.

I now pass on, and remark that there were at this time other weighty matters to which I gave some little thought, but of these I will not treat abstractedly, especially as it will equally well answer my purpose to notice them in a way which probably will be more acceptable to the reader. An opportunity for hinting at them will perhaps offer itself in the subjoined account of a venerable friend, of whom, after an intercourse of about thirty years, I was recently bereaved. I shall not err if I call him

A HAPPY MAN.

To him I became known through the agency of one who was *his* friend, as well as *mine*. He was about twenty years older than myself. Being observant and well informed, as also judicious and unquestionably religious, he was well qualified to be both my instructor and exemplar. How much I owe him for his good counsels and instructive examples I cannot say, but I hold myself considerably his debtor. He was of French origin, his first known ancestor having come from that country in the service of an English nobleman. His immediate ancestors were farmers, and he was of like occupation. His wife was a woman of almost surprising goodness of disposition, and remarkable both for good sense and prudent deportment. His children were well governed, and, moreover, were willing to be governed. Thus his house was indeed a happy home. I question whether a more delightful spectacle of domestic peace and unity has ever been witnessed. My revered friend was of a grave, yet cheerful, temper; thoroughly contented with his lot amidst all its vicissitudes, some of which were not a little perplexing and detrimental to his worldly interests. I never heard him complain of either the weather, the crops, or the state of the markets. One, who was necessarily far better acquainted with his habitual temper than I could be, has told me that she never knew him give any sign of vexation or discontent on any occasion whatever. He was an exemplary Christian, a member of the Church of England, to which Church he was, upon principle, warmly attached; yet he manifested a spirit of thorough good will to the members of other communions; indeed, I believe him to have been incapable of any feeling contrary to genuine Christian charity. Thus, for example, he thought that Dissenters would be far less hostile to our National Establishment, did they duly remember the divine declaration that kings and queens should eventually be made the nursing-fathers and nursing-mothers of the Christian Church. On the other hand, he believed that Churchmen are bound to avoid all angry controversies with Dissenters, and that they ought to aim at regarding them with feelings of genuine good will. He was further of opinion, that all clergymen who cannot conscientiously and unreservedly preach the doctrines, or conform to the discipline, of the Church, ought, as a matter of stern duty, to resign their livings.

In respect to national education, he thought that the State not only *might*, but also that it *should*, provide the means of giving it, and, further, that it should superintend the appropriation of those means, so far at least as to see that they are impartially distributed and faithfully applied. Moreover, he believed it to be the duty of all Christians, both clergy and laymen, to put aside all party feelings and opinions, in order that they might be at liberty to unite cordially in the great work of popular instruction.

Having been, under the former poor-law, a parish overseer, and under the new law a guardian of the poor, he was well qualified to give an opinion as to their comparative merits. His opinion was, that while the former poor-law was not sufficiently strict in its provisions, and was often administered in an improper manner, the new law is, in some respects, too harsh and indiscriminate. For himself, he had the satisfaction of knowing that he executed his office in a manner which gained him both the approbation of his colleagues and the good will of the poor on whose behalf he acted. In regard to political matters he was a Conservative, yet he never indulged in unfriendly feelings towards those who held opposite opinions. In his estimate of public men and public measures he had respect only to the conduct of the one, and the tendency of the other. If he believed that the men in office were governed by good principles, and that their measures were adapted to be useful, he was quite satisfied.

Thus, in every relation of life my deceased friend was exemplary. I do not presume to affirm that he was faultless; but I can safely avow that I never saw anything wrong in his demeanour, nor heard him utter a word that indicated a blameworthy feeling. He was in the habit of making periodical journeys to London, and thus I had the pleasure of seeing him once or twice in each year. The days on which he visited us were cheerful days, made so by his simple manners and pleasant conversation. He had visited us once during the year 1849; and we were looking for a second visit, when, instead of seeing him, we were informed of his recent and unexpected decease. Henceforth, if I would look upon him, it must be by the agency of the inward eye—the eye of the imagination. That I shall thus endeavour to see him, both as he appeared when here, and as I believe he now appears, I cannot doubt. Even while I am recording this brief account of him, I seem as though I could see his tall and spare form, bending under the weight of threescore and eighteen years, and, moreover, could hear his well-known and welcome voice. Had I leisure for musing, I should hardly fail to aim at bringing him within the range of my imaginative visual power.

Here, however, I must for the present turn from him, for, while writing these lines, I am apprised of the unexpected decease of that friend to whom I have more than once alluded in this volume. He was suddenly called away, and I cannot but be greatly moved at the departure of one with whom, for so many consecutive years, I had held free and unbroken correspondence.

Thus "friend after friend departs," and I naturally begin to look for the day when, if I remain in this life, I shall stand alone like a withered tree in the midst of a desolate and dreary wilderness. Yet I am neither alarmed nor saddened by the prospect. Through Divine mercy I am enabled to contemplate, without any painful emotion, the loneliness which seems to await me; while, by the same mercy, I have been made to regard the day of what is called "death" as being but the birthday of a deathless life.

Here I had thought to have said to the reader Farewell! but I cannot do so until I have told him that, since I wrote the foregoing paragraph, I have been apprised of the departure hence of two more of the friends of my early years. They were men well worthy of the good esteem in which they were generally held. Each was a self-taught yet well-informed man. They were equally exemplary for industry, tepmerance, prudence, and contentedness. Had I the "pen of a ready writer," I should probably give some particular account of each, as also of the much-valued friends noticed above; but, for the present, I must be satisfied with having paid to their memories these slight tributes of my esteem.

I have now but one more remark to make, and that applies to the reader. To him I recomm the above examples, and am bold to say, "Go do thou likewise."

THE END.

PRINTED BY W. CLOWES AND SONS, STAMFORD STREET.

www.ingramcontent.com/pod-product-compliance
Lightning Source LLC
Chambersburg PA
CBHW080434110426
42743CB00016B/3163